CW00570822

MORRIS L. VENDEN

THE ANSWER IS
Prayer

Pacific Press® Publishing Association
Nampa, Idaho
Oshawa, Ontario, Canada

Edited by Marvin Moore
Cover design by Michelle C. Petz
Cover image copyright © 1999 PhotoDisc, Inc.

Library of Congress Catalog Number: 88-62626

ISBN 0-8163-1120-X

99 00 01 • 12 11 10 9

Contents

Chapter 1
The Problem With Prayer

My wife and I had the privilege of traveling with Elder H. M. S. Richards, Sr., on the last tour group he took to the Holy Land. One of the places we visited was the tomb where many scholars believe Christ was buried.

We took turns going inside the little stone room, and I can still remember H. M. S. Richards coming to the door and saying to those of us outside, "He's not there! It's empty!"

Buddha is dead. Mohammed is dead. You can still visit their remains. But when you go to the tomb of Christ, it's empty. The Christian religion can be distinguished from all other world religions by the fact that it claims to worship a *living* God. We do not base our faith on some creed or a collection of wisdom written down long ago. We do not join the heathen worshipers who bow to idols of wood and stone. Our God is alive! As Francis Schaeffer's book title proclaims, *He Is There and He Is Not Silent*.

But this brings us to a problem. Prayer doesn't always work out the way we expect it to. In spite of the fact that we claim to believe in a God who is alive, a God who is there, a God who is love, we often find that He does not respond to our prayers in any way that we can measure.

Sometimes I ask groups of Christians to indicate how many of them can remember a specific, definite answer to prayer. It's amazing how many are unable to think of a single one!

Once when I was a child, my kite got caught in a tree. In my hour of need I prayed that God would get my kite out of the tree. Then I watched from below, holding on to the string, while the kite moved gently back and forth through the branches of the tree. Suddenly it broke free, unharmed. I knew God heard my prayer that day!

Perhaps you once had a similar experience, but forgot about it. Yet even the fact that some answers to prayer have been forgotten is in itself significant: Because far more of our prayers seem to go unanswered, that's what we remember best.

Of course, as Christians we aren't supposed to believe in unanswered prayer, so we come up with all sorts of rationales to explain our disappointment. We say, "Sometimes God says Yes, sometimes He says No, and sometimes He says to wait awhile." Or we say, "The answer may not come in the way we expect." Sometimes we say, "God will answer Yes to prayer only when it is according to His will."

But in the end, many Christians find themselves just a little suspicious of the process of prayer. They've been burned too many times. So they continue going through the routine of "prayer," but their requests are so general that they can never be sure whether their prayers were answered.

Have you ever listened to a prayer like this?

Dear heavenly Father, We ask for Your presence here with us this morning. Give us understanding hearts, that we may learn what You want us to know. Be with the sick and afflicted and those who are not here with us this morning. Bless the missionaries and the colporteurs in the foreign fields. Guide in the affairs of government. And at last, when You come, grant that we, without the loss of one, may gain an abundant entrance into Your kingdom. For we ask it all in Jesus' name, Amen.

Now tell me. If God were to answer that prayer by saying Yes, what would you get? How would you know that He had responded?

Yet we are often afraid to pray more specifically, especially in public, because we remember the times when it seemed that our prayers weren't answered, and we remember what that did to us on the inside—what it did to our faith in a God of love. To avoid letting that happen again, we make prayer a routine, a ritual, a last resort.

Perhaps you heard about the two people who were discussing a friend's crisis. The first described all the things that had been tried but hadn't helped, and finally said, "It looks like there's nothing left to do but pray."

To which the second responded, "Alas! Has it come to *that*?"

We smile at such stories. But we *live* them. We believe in prayer. Yes, go ahead. It can't hurt anything to pray about it. But when it comes to the bottom line, we have a lot more faith in our own work than we do in God's work for us.

We start our children out with a stiff diet of Daniel in the lions' den, the Hebrew worthies in the fiery furnace, and Moses crossing the Red Sea with the Egyptians hot on his trail. We put them to bed with stories of Elijah on Mount Carmel and Abraham on Mount Moriah, the knife in his upraised hand. But the first time their childish faith puts God to the test, we cringe in fear.

My wife and I were living in Glendale, California, when our children were small. Brush fires were blazing nearby, and the police evacuated our area. We were obviously worried as we awaited the outcome from a safe distance, but the children said, "Don't worry, Daddy. Our house won't burn. We prayed and asked God to protect it."

Has anything like that ever happened to you? Have you ever had car trouble, and your children in the backseat said, "Why don't we ask Jesus to start the car"?

Have you ever lost something important, and after hunting everywhere had your children suggest, "Let's pray and ask Jesus to find it for us"? It puts you in a hard place, doesn't it?

As a Christian parent, you can't exactly see your way clear to say, "Don't bother praying. *That* surely won't do any good!"

Yet neither can you find an explanation that will satisfy your children (and yourself) if the house does burn or the car fails to start or you don't find the missing item.

So you tell the children, "Maybe it wasn't *God's will* to keep the house from burning or to start the car." If that's true, then maybe it would be better just to pray, "Please be with us and help us." That way it won't be so noticeable if there's no answer!

Yet while all this is going on you find yourself begging God, "Come on, please, answer this one for the kiddies. They're too young to . . ."

To *what*—discover that God isn't really what you've told them He is? To discover that prayer doesn't really "work" after all? We're so afraid that our children might ask questions for which we have no answers!

There's another factor that haunts us when it comes to prayer: sin. We've been told that God doesn't hear sinners. We've learned that it's our iniquities that separate us and God so that He does not hear us. Every time we consider calling to Him in prayer, the devil is on hand with an up-to-date list of reasons why we would be wasting our breath.

Silence from God is one of our greatest problems with prayer. When we distinguish between effective prayer and ineffective prayer, we mean prayer that brings a response versus prayer that brings no response. We know that God, being omniscient and omnipresent, *hears* every word that we utter, in prayer or otherwise. So when we speak of His "hearing" our prayers, we expect a response on His part. He must not only hear, but He must act because of what He hears.

It's true that prayer is primarily for communication, not just to get answers. But communication insists on a two-way street. Have you ever been talking to someone, sharing something that was important to you, and gotten no response? What's the first thing you asked? You said, "Are you listening?" Effective communication requires a response.

So it's natural, when we communicate with God, to expect a response. But remember this: "Response" can mean more than just getting your requests granted. God's response can come in other forms.

The search of the Christian in the study of prayer is to define and then to experience effectual prayer. We want to learn what makes the difference and how to avoid prayer that is ineffective. We want to be in touch with a God who has promised not only to hear, but to respond.

When we question why prayer does not always bring the response we seek or expect, we are not alone. Consider Job's lament:

> Then Job replied: "Even today my complaint is bitter; his hand is heavy in spite of my groaning. If only I knew where to find him; if only I could go to his dwelling! I would state my case before him and fill my mouth with arguments. I would find out what he would answer me, and consider what he would say. Would he oppose me with great power? No, he would not press charges against me. There an upright man could present his case before him, and I would be delivered forever from my judge. But if I go to the east, he is not there; if I go to the west, I do not find him. When he is at work in the north, I do not see him; When he turns to the south, I catch no glimpse of him" (Job 23: 1-9, NIV).

David prayed, "Keep not thou silence, O God: hold not thy peace, and be not still, O God" (Psalm 83:1). Even for Christ, when He was on the cross and experiencing the silence of God, came the question, "My God, my God, why have you forsaken me?" (Mark 15:24, NIV).

So when it appears that God is not responding to your prayers, you are in good company. Yet is it possible that He longs to respond far more than we permit Him to? Is there more available in our two-way communication with God than most of us have experienced? How are we to deal with the times when God is silent? What is He saying to us as He "speaks" to us through that very silence? These are questions for which we are seeking solutions. The goal of this study is to learn more about communication with God through prayer, so that we may learn to know Him better and trust Him more.

Chapter 2
Kinds of Prayer

Someone once said that when we talk to God, it's prayer; but when God talks to us, it's schizophrenia. In no other area of life do we seek so eagerly for a response, and view the response with such suspicion when we get it! But the major premise of this book is that God responds. He not only listens; He replies.

That doesn't mean He always says Yes, though if you study the prayers of the Bible carefully, you will find that the ones where the answer was No are in the minority. With only a few exceptions, prayers in the Bible received a definite, positive response within a short enough time that it was obvious God had responded. So let's nail it down to begin with: When you pray, you can expect God to answer.

However, God's response may differ, depending on the type of prayer you offer. So let's take some time to examine the various types of prayer, and the kind of response we can expect when we pray.

We might classify prayer according to its various *forms*, such as silent prayer, private or secret prayer, public prayer, family or group prayer, and so on. It's true that we are invited to come to God in prayer both privately and in association with others. But there is a deeper way to think about prayer than simply who is involved in making the petition.

We will begin with the more common types of prayer, and progress to those that are less well known.

Prayers of Repentance and Confession

It is through a prayer of repentance and confession that we come to Christ in the first place, admitting that we are sinners and accepting His justifying grace. This is familiar ground for most Christians.

Perhaps the most outstanding Bible example of this type of prayer is David's prayer in Psalm 51. In fact, this has been called the Penitential Psalm. David had sinned greatly: covetousness, deceit, adultery, murder—he had added one sin to another, until finally the prophet Nathan was sent to stop him in his downward rush. David's sin was great, but so was his repentance. Notice his words:

> Have mercy upon me, O God, according to thy lovingkindness: according unto the multitude of thy tender mercies blot out my transgressions. Wash me thoroughly from mine iniquity, and cleanse me from my sin. For I acknowledge my transgressions: and my sin is ever before me (Psalm 51:1-3).

Have you ever found yourself trapped in a downward spiral of sin, unable to see a way to escape? Here's the first step, which is so simple that it might easily be overlooked: Admit that you have a problem! Jeremiah 3:13 says it: "Only acknowledge thine iniquity, that thou hast transgressed against the Lord thy God."

David made that confession, admitting that he had sinned and was in desperate need of God's mercy and forgiveness. Then he continued: "Against thee, thee only, have I sinned, and done this evil in thy sight" (verse 4).

Wait a minute! Hadn't David sinned against Bathsheba? Hadn't he sinned against her husband Uriah, and against his own family? Hadn't he sinned against the captain in the army to whom he delegated the responsibility for carrying out his murderous designs? Hadn't he sinned against the entire house of Israel in not living up to his high calling as the king anointed by God to rule over them? Of course he had.

But David recognized that his first and greatest sin was against God Himself. When he saw himself in the light of his relationship to God, he recognized how guilty he really was. He prayed:

> Hide thy face from my sins, and blot out all mine iniquities. Create in me a clean heart, O God; and renew a right spirit within me. Cast me not away from thy presence; and take not thy holy spirit from me. Restore unto me the joy of thy salvation; and uphold me with thy free spirit (verses 9-12).

David was truly sorry, not only for the consequences of his evil deeds, but primarily for the sorrow he had brought to the heart of God. His repentance was sincere and genuine.

The Bible gives a number of examples of this type of prayer. Daniel prayed a prayer of repentance and confession, not just for himself but on behalf of all God's people:

> We have sinned, and have committed iniquity, and have done wickedly, and have rebelled, even by departing from thy precepts and from thy judgments: neither have we hearkened unto thy servants the prophets, which spake in thy name to our kings, our princes, and our fathers, and to all the people of the land. O Lord, righteousness belongeth unto thee, but unto us confusion of faces, as at this day (Daniel 9:5-7).

When we see the righteousness that belongs alone to God, we are brought to see ourselves in a true light. Only then can we pray in true repentance and confession.

Ezra confessed the sins of the people of Israel. He felt so grieved at the wickedness of the people of his day that he said, "When I heard this thing, I rent my garment and my mantle, and plucked off the hair of my head and of my beard, and sat down astonied" (Ezra 9:3). Ezra was pretty upset, wasn't he? Finally, at the time of the evening sacrifice, he began to pray:

O my God, I am ashamed and blush to lift up my face to thee, my God: For our iniquities are increased over our head, and our trespass is grown up unto the heavens (verse 6).

These are just a few examples of prayers of repentance and confession in the Bible.

When we come to God with our prayers of repentance and confession, like Ezra, we may feel ashamed and blush to even approach Him in our wretched condition. Because we don't *feel* any different, we may fear that He has not heard and responded to our requests for His mercy and forgiveness. But God does not keep His promises on the basis of our feelings. He has already given us His Word what His response will be when we come to Him for forgiveness. The answer is always Yes. Immediately.

Jesus said it in John 6:37: "Him that cometh to me I will in no wise cast out." Any time we come to Him, we are always, *always* accepted. No matter how many times we have turned from Him, any time we turn back and seek His forgiveness, He is waiting to accept us once again.

So what is God's response to prayers of repentance and confession? He forgives and accepts us. He forgives, and more than that, He covers us with His righteousness so that we stand before Him as though we had never, ever even sinned.

Prayers of Request

Requests are probably the most common form of prayer. Sometimes we turn God into Santa Claus. Our prayer life consists almost entirely of asking and receiving.

This wouldn't work if you tried it on your human friends. How long would any relationship last if every time you talked to that person you said, "And would you please give me this and do that for me and take care of the other"? Perhaps it was in reaction against this brand of Christianity that Calvin Miller wrote in *The Philippian Fragment*, "Where is the one who asks for nothing because he already has everything?"

Matthew 6:33 says it: "Seek ye first the kingdom of God, and his righteousness; and all these things shall be added unto you." So our first seeking for God should always be for spiritual communion rather than for temporal blessings.

However, the Bible does invite prayers of request. Abraham asked for a son. Did he get a response? Yes, he did. Joshua focused on the sun, too—a different sun this time! He also received the answer that he requested, and the sun stood still while he finished his battle with the enemy.

Many Bible prayer requests have to do with healing. Matthew 9 tells about Jairus, who asked Jesus to come and heal his daughter. By the time Jesus arrived, the daughter had already died, but that was no problem for Him. Jairus's daughter was restored to him that very day. The Syrophoenician woman asked Jesus to heal her daughter, who was grievously vexed with a devil. Did she get a response? Yes. Jesus appeared to ignore her request for a time, but then He granted her desire.

The Bible teaches that prayer requests *are* answered! The overwhelming majority of the prayer requests that are recorded in the Bible were not only answered, but were answered Yes. And where the answer was No an explanation was given. When God denied Paul's request to remove the thorn in his flesh, He said, "No—My grace is sufficient." When He denied Moses' request to enter the land of Canaan, He said, "No—you cannot enter because of your sin. And don't ask Me anymore!" When God denied David's request to build a temple in His honor, He said, "No—you are a man of blood. Your son will build it instead." Usually the refusal was because the honor, glory, and reputation of God were at stake.

There was often a delay in God's response to Bible prayers, but when His answer was Wait, He made up for the delay by extra help in order to keep the person's faith strong while he or she waited. He invited His people to keep on asking until they received a definite response one way or the other.

Prayers of Thanksgiving and Praise

The Bible is filled with prayers of thanksgiving and praise.

Our problem as Christians is that we often neglect this type of prayer. Yet God is worthy of our praise, is He not?

Remember when you were small and someone did you a favor or gave you a gift? Almost before you had a chance to open your mouth your parents said, "What do you say?" They hoped that before too many years passed, you would remember to say Thank you on your own, without someone prompting you!

What about saying Thank You to the Creator of the universe, who keeps your heart beating and who daily loads you with benefits? How long has it been since you made a special point of saying Thank You to Him?

It was a wonderful day when the Red Sea parted and the children of Israel went through on dry ground. They praised God in song with these words:

> I will sing unto the Lord, for he hath triumphed gloriously: the horse and his rider hath he thrown into the sea. The Lord is my strength and song, and he is become my salvation: he is my God, and I will prepare him an habitation; my father's God, and I will exalt him (Exodus 15:1, 2).

The Israelites continued to sing and praise the wonders that the Lord had accomplished for them that day. They were encouraged to keep that day in memory, to recount the story of their deliverance from Egypt through the coming years as a reminder to their children and their children's children of the blessings and goodness of the Lord to them. You can read one such recounting in Deuteronomy 26.

The Psalms are filled with praises to God. Psalm 50:14 says, "Offer unto God thanksgiving." Psalm 57:9-11 says, "I will praise thee, O Lord, among the people: I will sing unto thee among the nations. For thy mercy is great unto the heavens, and thy truth unto the clouds. Be thou exalted, O God, above the heavens: let thy glory be above all the earth." Psalm 107:1 says, "O give thanks unto the Lord, for he is good: for his mercy endureth for ever." And so on, and on, and on. The writers of the Psalms never seemed to tire of exalting the name of God and praising Him for His goodness and mercy.

Isaiah gives a prayer of praise to God that begins with these words: "O Lord, thou art my God; I will exalt thee, I will praise thy name; for thou hast done wonderful things; thy counsels of old are faithfulness and truth" (Isaiah 25:1). Jeremiah praised by saying, "Ah Lord God! behold, thou hast made the heaven and the earth by thy great power and stretched out arm, and there is nothing too hard for thee" (Jeremiah 32:17).

Jesus praised His Father and publicly thanked Him for hearing and answering His prayers. At the tomb of Lazarus He said, "Father, I thank thee that thou hast heard me. And I knew that thou hearest me always: but because of the people which stand by I said it, that they may believe that thou hast sent me" (John 11:41, 42).

Right through to the last book of the Bible, the book of Revelation, praise and thanksgiving to God are offered continually. Revelation 5:12 says, "Worthy is the Lamb that was slain to receive power, and riches, and wisdom, and strength, and honour, and glory, and blessing." And in Revelation 19:6 the voice of the great multitude is heard saying, "Alleluia: for the Lord God omnipotent reigneth."

We will take a longer look at the subject of prayer and praise later, but for now let's notice God's response to prayers of praise and thanksgiving. Does He respond?

Paul and Silas praised God with song at midnight, in spite of the fact that they were in jail. Do you remember the story? There was a mighty earthquake! How do you like that for a response? It was so dramatic it was almost frightening. The jailer was so afraid that he was ready to put his sword through his heart, but the apostles called out to him, "Don't harm yourself! We are all here!" (Acts 16:28, NIV).

In Acts 4 you can find the story of a church that prayed, praising God for His might and power, and God said, "You're right. Here's a sample." And again there was an earthquake. Evidently God enjoys earthquakes!

When people praise God and give Him thanks, sometimes He responds in a visible way. At other times His response may be the joy of a singing heart.

Prayer for Guidance

Little did Gideon know, when he took his fleece and left it outside overnight, that his act would be published abroad for thousands of years to come! The story of Gideon is one of the best-known Bible examples of prayer for guidance. Gideon needed to know for certain what God's will was for his life at that time, and he asked not only for a response from God, but for a particular form of response, which God saw fit to honor.

The three Hebrew worthies, and Daniel himself, suddenly found themselves in a crisis (see Daniel 2). Apparently the first knowledge they were given about the king's demand for an interpretation for his forgotten dream was when the soldiers showed up at their door to lead them off to the execution! They asked for enough time to consult their God, and God responded, revealing the king's secrets unto them by means of a dream.

Sometimes immature Christians have out-Gideoned Gideon! Their prayers for guidance become one set of signs after another as they try to manufacture methods for God to communicate His will to them. Yet even for Gideon, this particular structuring of God's response was apparently a one-time experience. Far more common, in Bible prayer stories, is for someone to request that God will give them a sign, but then leave it up to Him to determine what that sign should be.

The subject of understanding the guidance of God is a big one, which I have discussed much more completely in the book, *How to Know God's Will in Your Life.* For our purposes here, we will simply underline one point: God wants to guide and instruct His people. His response to their prayers for guidance may be sent in a variety of ways. He may choose to work through signs or through His will as revealed in His Word. He may communicate through providential circumstances or through open and closed doors. He may send conviction from the Holy Spirit to give an inner sense of His will for us, or He may work through other Christians to share with us the benefit of their experience, wisdom, and understanding. In most cases, God works through several or all of these methods, so that when we look at the total picture, we understand His will for us in a given situation because of the weight of evidence.

But God responds! We are not limited to praying for guidance, and then making our decisions based on our own judgment, knowledge, and common sense. If that were all that were needed to make a right choice or decision, then the atheist would have no disadvantage in choosing the right way! God wants to guide His people, and we are safe in waiting and watching for Him to respond. Consider this paragraph from the book *Prophets and Kings*:

> The records of sacred history are written, not merely that we may read and wonder, but that the same faith which wrought in God's servants of old may work in us. In no less marked manner will the Lord work now, wherever there are hearts of faith to be channels of His power (page 175).

Devotional Prayers

How did Jesus manage to spend so much time in prayer—even entire nights, when He would become so absorbed in communion with His Father that He would forget to go to bed? Have you ever tried to imagine what He prayed about? Let's look at the types of prayer we have considered so far. Jesus had no need for repentance and confession, so He did not pray for that. However, He had requests that He brought before the Father—requests for the needs He felt as a human being, experiencing the weaknesses that are common to mankind. He must have spent time in thanksgiving and praise, and we are told that He sought for guidance from above in the same way we are to seek it, as day by day He waited for His Father to make known the plans for His life. *The Desire of Ages* tells us that Jesus made no plans for Himself, but received them day by day from His Father. You can read it on page 208:

> The Son of God was surrendered to the Father's will, and dependent upon His power. So utterly was Christ emptied of self that He made no plans for Himself. He accepted God's plans for Him, and day by day the Father

unfolded His plans. So should we depend upon God, that our lives may be the simple outworking of His will.

But no matter what the nature of the requests Jesus presented before the Father, and no matter how often He returned thanks to the Father for His love and care, He must have spent the majority of His time just talking. He knew the secret of talking to God as to a Friend.

And how do we talk to friends? Why, we just talk! We share what's on our minds. We discuss what's happening in our lives. We talk about how we feel and what we think. We share our concerns and our joys. Communication with a friend goes far beyond asking for favors and expressing appreciation for favors received.

Devotional prayer is talking to God the way you would to a friend. Have you ever tried it? Have you ever read a chapter from *The Desire of Ages* or a passage of Scripture and deliberately tried to put yourself in the picture, praying as you read, praying about what you read? If so, you have had the opportunity of hearing God's response. He guides your thoughts. He shows you how the story you are reading applies to your own life and needs.

Then, if you ever slowed down enough to let your soul catch up with your body, you may have learned the secret of not rushing off to work or business once you finish your part of the conversation. You wait. You listen with your mind. Many people have discovered that God guides their thoughts in a personal, specific way, communicating to them in the quiet of their own hearts.

Devotional prayer can be two-way in an even more exciting way than the usual request and response. As we slow down and take the time to commune with God, He will respond in communion with us. He is willing to spend just as much time in fellowship with us as we are willing to spend with Him. We are always the ones who set the limits on the relationship. He never does.

"He will speak His mysteries to us personally. Our hearts will often burn within us as One draws nigh to commune with us as He did with Enoch" (*The Desire of Ages* p. 668).

"We may be admitted into closet intimacy and communion with God" (*Mount of Blessing* p. 131).

Intercessory Prayer

Intercessory prayer is the one type of prayer that God delights to answer above all others. He may not be able to grant your requests as freely when you seek His blessings for yourself, because your own selfishness may get mixed up in the process. But when you pray for others, you are joining with the great Intercessor. Jesus prayed for others more than for Himself (see *The Desire of Ages*, p. 379). He prayed for you! You can read His prayer for you in John 17. And as you join Him in His ministry of intercession for others, somehow you will be drawn nearer to Him yourself.

Moses interceded for the people of Israel over and over again. We remember best his classic prayer when he offered his own eternal life for the lives of the people if that would somehow make a difference. This pattern was repeated many times throughout their journey from Egypt to Canaan. The people would reach a crisis. They would groan and complain and grumble, and Moses would go to his knees in their behalf.

Sometimes people try to say that prayer is primarily of value as a catharsis and that a person could receive the same benefit by "talking it out" with a friend or counselor, or perhaps even his dog! But one of the evidences that prayer works is that when we pray for others, even without their knowledge, our prayers make a difference.

The subject of intercessory prayer is an exciting one, and we will spend an entire chapter on it later, but once again, the assurance of God's response is certain. In Luke 11:5-13, where Jesus gave a parable about intercessory prayer, we see someone going at midnight to plead for bread for a friend. He didn't need it for himself—his family had already eaten and been filled. But a friend had come to him with a need. And so he pleaded, even in the face of apparent denial, until his request was granted.

The parable doesn't end with the needs of the friend being

left unmet. The friend doesn't go to bed hungry, even though the hour is late. Bread is given to meet the emergency. What a wonderful assurance that is to us of God's willingness to bless, particularly when we seek a blessing for those around us!

Dialogue Prayer

Finally, we must look briefly at the least common type of prayer: dialogue prayer. The Bible records a number of times when God actually entered into conversation with His people. Most of us, even Christians, are very uncomfortable with this idea of prayer, and therefore have had little if any experience with it. Perhaps we even run from it!

It differs from the other types of prayer in that it is asking from God a response that is direct, immediate, and specific to the subject that we are bringing to His attention. It is less asking God to *act*, and more asking Him to *talk* to us about His actions before He acts. It also allows God, at times, to take the initiative in the subject of the conversation or to choose the subject of the conversation altogether.

It's almost frightening to consider dialogue prayer, even briefly! Yet if we are to be objective in examining the various kinds of prayer in the Bible, we must include this one.

Abraham experienced this kind of prayer when he prayed for Sodom (see Genesis 18 and 19). He finally realized who had been to dinner, and when God shared some of His confidences with Abraham about His plans for Sodom, Abraham began to talk back! Abraham didn't choose the subject of the conversation—God initiated it. Surely God knew what sort of material He was dealing with, and He knew what Abraham's response would be. He invited Abraham to talk about it so that He could explain His judgments and Abraham could understand.

Moses engaged in this kind of prayer several times. At the burning bush, he argued with God about his qualifications for being the leader of the Exodus movement (see Exodus 3 and 4). Again, God set up the interview. Moses was minding his own business, there on the backside of the mountain. He had no intention of leading an exodus from Egypt—he was busy herding sheep! For him, the day at the burning bush began just the same as any other day. He didn't realize that God was waiting for him, looking for a chance to talk.

Jacob dialogued with God in prayer after he got in a fight with Jesus at the brook Jabbok (see Genesis 32). After the night of wrestling by the brook, when the morning dawned and Jacob realized who he had been fighting with, he engaged his Opponent in conversation. You remember the story. Jesus said, "Let me go." But instead of letting go Jacob said, "Wait just a minute!" And he hung on tight, refusing to let go, refusing to give up. Ellen White tells us that it was Christ Himself who gave Jacob the courage and determination to hang on—and that's good news too, isn't it? (see *Christ's Object Lessons*, p. 175).

There are other examples in the Bible of this type of prayer, and perhaps before the turning of the last few pages of this earth's history, we will know more of it in our own day.

Sometimes people try to explain the miracles and angel visits, the visions and dreams of Bible times by saying, "Well, they needed it more back then, but now we are more enlightened, and so God doesn't have to stoop to such measures." But if we understand anything at all about the cumulative effects of sin over the years upon the human organism, then we realize that we are *more* in need of the manifestations of God's power than were the people of Bible times!

And the promise is given that in the last days the more open lines of communication will be revived. Joel talks about dreaming dreams and seeing visions in the time of the end. Notice also this paragraph by Ellen White:

Will he who with his divine finger drew the boundaries of Judea, who designated the exact spot where the temple should stand, who wrought out designs for the Jewish church and for the service of the sanctuary, leave his people, his chosen people, who keep his commandments, to a chance experience, to accident, to stumble along in darkness? Shall those to whom he has committed most precious light, to whom he has intrusted the third angel's message, have less of his providential leading than had his ancient people? (*Review and Herald*, Feb. 21, 1893).

God *wants* to communicate with us, whatever the method He chooses. John 14:21 says it: "I will love him, and will manifest myself to him." John 15:15 says it: "Henceforth I call you not servants; for the servant knoweth not what his lord doeth: but I have called you friends." John 10:4, 5 says it: "He goeth before them, and the sheep follow him: for they know his voice. And a stranger will they not follow, but will flee from him: for they know not the voice of strangers."

Jesus gave these promises to His disciples, but the promise is for us as well. *The Desire of Ages*, page 669, says: "By the Spirit the Saviour would be accessible to all. In this sense He would be nearer to them than if He had not ascended on high." So instead of expecting to have less of His presence today, we have been given the promise of even more.

In the book *Steps to Christ* are these encouraging words:

"The Lord is very pitiful and of tender mercy." . . . His heart of love is touched by our sorrows and even by our utterances of them. Take to Him everything that perplexes the mind. Nothing is too great for Him to bear, for He holds up worlds. He rules over all the affairs of the universe. Nothing that in any way concerns our peace is too small for Him to notice. There is no chapter in our experience too dark for Him to read; there is no perplexity too difficult for Him to unravel. No calamity can befall the least of His children, no anxiety harass the soul, no joy cheer, no sincere prayer escape the lips, of which our heavenly Father is unobservant, or in which He takes no immediate interest. "He healeth the broken in heart, and bindeth up their wounds." . . . The relations between God and each soul are as distinct and full as though there were not another soul upon the earth to share His watchcare, not another soul for whom He gave His beloved Son (p. 100).

Chapter 3
Why Pray?

Brent and Nancy were friends with the mayor of their town. They had known him personally for a number of years and had often enjoyed his company in their home. Every time he ran for office they were active helpers in his campaigns, and they voted for him at election time. They passed out handbills, helped with his political rallies, and shared with others all the good reasons they could think of why everyone should vote for their friend as town mayor. Every time he was reelected, they joined in the victory celebrations with great enthusiasm.

Next door to Brent and Nancy lived old Mr. Perkins. Mr. Perkins hated the mayor, and he let everybody know it. Everything that went wrong in their town, he blamed directly on the mayor. If the price of gasoline went up a few cents or if the bus was running late or if the dog across the street chased his cat, Mr. Perkins was sure it was the mayor's fault. He blamed the mayor for the tree roots blocking his sewer lines and for the cracks in his sidewalk. He had voted against the mayor in every election, and he was proud of it!

He particularly delighted in taunting Brent and Nancy for their friendship with the mayor. When he passed them on the sidewalk he would say things like, "Too bad your friend the mayor can't do something about the lack of parking spaces uptown." Or, "My social security check was late again this month—but what can you expect, with your friend the mayor trying to run things around here?"

One evening, when the mayor had come to their house for

dinner, they were all looking out the front window. Mr. Perkins came walking along toward his house, saw the mayor's car, and stopped. He looked at the car, looked toward the house, and scowled. Then he went over to the mayor's car and *spit* directly on the gleaming windshield!

Brent and Nancy were outraged. "You should have him arrested!" exclaimed Brent.

"Evict him from his house," suggested Nancy. "Get the town to turn his lot into a park or something! Don't you see how he treats you?"

But the mayor did nothing.

Then one day it began to rain. Day after day it rained, heavily, steadily. The town had never gotten this much rain before! The streets and basements were flooded. Water stood in pools in the gardens and sidewalks. And still the rain continued. At last the dam broke, and the river's current came rushing through the streets. In the neighborhood where Brent and Nancy lived, all the homes were swept away. Only their lives were saved. Everything they owned was lost to the waters of the flood.

As soon as the rains ended and the flood waters began to recede, it was announced that funding was available through the mayor's office for those who had lost their homes in the flood. An announcement was printed in the town newspaper that applications would be taken at the mayor's office, and the funds would be distributed to those in need of assistance.

Brent and Nancy felt relieved. They never worried for a minute after that. They were sure that their friend, the mayor, would see to it that they received the full amount as soon as possible, so that their home could be rebuilt and they could replace their lost possessions. Confidently, they took their application to the mayor himself and left it in his hands.

Then they waited. And waited. And waited some more. Several weeks went by. "I wonder why it's taking so long," Brent said one day. "I thought surely we would have had the money before now."

"There must be some good reason," Nancy replied. "Aren't we lucky that *we* don't have to worry? This is a good time to be friends with the mayor!"

"I sure wouldn't want to be in Mr. Perkins's shoes right now," added Brent. "I wonder if he even bothered to put in an application."

A few more weeks went by. Still they received no response. Then one day the newspaper ran a special article on the flood victims and showed a picture of guess who? That's right! Mr. Perkins—standing in front of his newly framed house.

Brent and Nancy hurried over to their old neighborhood to see for themselves. Sure enough, when they reached their block, there was Mr. Perkins working on his house.

They went over to where he was working and greeted him.

Mr. Perkins growled, "If your friend the mayor had been tending to his business and had had the dam repaired, we wouldn't be in this mess. It took him long enough to get us the money to rebuild too. It was over a week before I got mine."

"Uh, when did you put in your application?" asked Nancy.

"Never did," said Mr. Perkins. "The mayor ought to know who needs to have their house rebuilt. What did he need an application for?" Then he added, "I suppose you got yours right off the top, since you've been so thick with the mayor all these years. Why haven't you started to rebuild?"

"We haven't gotten our money yet," said Brent. "We put in our application, though, and I'm sure there's some good reason why there's been a delay."

Mr. Perkins looked unbelievingly from Brent to Nancy, and back again. The he started laughing. He was still laughing as Brent and Nancy started slowly away. Finally he stopped just long enough to call out after them, "Now, aren't you glad you're friends with the mayor?"

Would you like to be friends with this mayor? Do you think it was worthwhile to put in an "application"? Have you ever found that God works the same way? Let's look at a few Scripture references that talk about how God treats His friends, and those who are not His friends. Jesus said:

But I say unto you, Love your enemies, bless them

that curse you, do good to them that hate you, and pray for them which despitefully use you, and persecute you; that ye may be the children of your Father which is in heaven: for he maketh his sun to rise on the evil and on the good, and sendeth rain on the just and on the unjust (Matthew 5:44, 45).

God could have chosen to be selective in bestowing His gift of light. He could have decided to work the way He did at the time of the Exodus, when for three days the people of Israel had light in their dwellings, but the Egyptians were in darkness. But instead, the general rule is that the sun and rain are given equally to all, regardless of their goodness or badness. We can nail it down, as a sort of axiom or thesis, that *God gives some blessings to good and bad alike.*

Jeremiah questioned God's dealing with the wicked:

Righteous art thou, O Lord, when I plead with thee: yet let me talk with thee of thy judgments: Wherefore doth the way of the wicked prosper? wherefore are all they happy that deal very treacherously? Thou hast planted them, yea, they have taken root: they grow, yea, they bring forth fruit (Jeremiah 12:1, 2).

Apparently Jeremiah wasn't unhappy with the response he received from God for his own needs, because he said, "Righteous art thou, O Lord, when I plead with thee." But he wanted God to be more careful with His blessings and swifter with His judgments.

David, on the other hand, discovered not only that God seemed willing to bless His enemies, but that His friends, such as David himself, seemed to be shortchanged in the blessing department. David found that the wicked were receiving blessings all along the way, while he suffered from trials, struggles, and afflictions. This discovery almost caused him to lose his faith in God:

I had nearly lost confidence; my faith was almost gone

because I was jealous of the proud when I saw that things go well for the wicked. They do not suffer pain; they are strong and healthy. They do not suffer as other people do; they do not have the troubles that others have. And so they wear pride like a necklace and violence like a robe; their hearts pour out evil, and their minds are busy with wicked schemes. They laugh at other people and speak of evil things; they are proud and make plans to oppress others. They speak evil of God in heaven and give arrogant orders to men on earth, so that even God's people turn to them and eagerly believe whatever they say. They say, "God will not know; the Most High will not find out." That is what the wicked are like. They have plenty and are always getting more. Is it for nothing, then, that I have kept myself pure and have not committed sin? O God, you have made me suffer all day long; every morning you have punished me (Psalm 73:2-14, TEV).

It is clear from these scriptures that God allows, and even sends, blessings and prosperity to those who despise His mercy; and it is also true that even those who are His children, who present their requests to Him in prayer, sometimes find that they have been denied. Do you have trouble with that? Welcome to the club! David and Jeremiah had the same problem. So did Job. So have many other godly people down through the ages.

But whether or not you have trouble with this truth, *it is still the truth*! It's another thesis that we can find in the study of prayer:

A lot of good things will happen to you, even if you don't pray; and a lot of bad things will happen to you even if you do pray.

Christians tend to believe that God's blessings are showered upon them because of their righteousness. But when they discover the truth about righteousness by faith in Christ alone and realize that it is within their relationship with God, through connection with Him, that they have their only hope of righteousness, they change their thinking. Then they decide that God's blessings are showered upon them because of their friendship with Him.

That makes sense. In our human experience, we have learned that there are benefits to having friends in high places. It can be worthwhile to be "friends with the mayor"! You expect more of your friends than you do of strangers or enemies. If you make an appeal to one who is your friend, you expect that your appeal will be given priority. That's what friends are for, right?

We expect God to send blessings to His friends, because they are His friends. When we discover, sooner or later, that some of God's blessings are showered upon His enemies because they are His enemies, we become confused.

The story is told of Abraham Lincoln's gracious treatment of his enemies. One of his aids wanted him to be more aggressive in fighting those who opposed him. He asked, "Why don't you destroy your enemies? Why do you always try to make friends with them?"

To which Lincoln replied, "Have I not destroyed my enemies if they have become my friends?"

Go back to the passage of Scripture we read earlier, where Jesus described how His Father sends the rain on the just and the unjust. He began by saying what? "Love your enemies, bless them that curse you, do good to them that hate you" (Matthew 5:44). And so on. Why are we told to treat our enemies in this way? So that we may be the children of our Father which is in heaven. In other words, that's the way God is. He showers blessings upon His enemies, *because* they are His enemies and He would like for them to become His friends. He loves His enemies as well as His friends. That's the good news of the gospel.

What is our response to a God like that? Do we say with David, "Is it for nothing, then, that I have kept myself pure and have not committed sin"? Wait a minute! Are we only friends with God because of what we hope to get out of Him? If that is our only reason for serving God—to try to gain His blessings for ourselves—then are we really His friends?

Let's go back to the parable about the friends of the mayor for a moment. If Brent and Nancy were truly friends with the mayor, would they be willing to wait for their turn, even if it wasn't "fair," while the mayor did everything he could do to become friends with Mr. Perkins? Would they be willing to give up their "rights" as the mayor's friend, so that those who were watching could see that the mayor didn't play favorites?

Is it possible that your Friend, the God of the universe, might need the same sort of support from His friends? Is it possible that, because of the accusations of the enemy, He sometimes allows His friends to wait, so it will be apparent to the entire universe that His friends truly love Him for Himself, and not just for what they hope to get out of Him?

An understanding of the great controversy can explain many of the things that would otherwise remain mysteries about God's dealing with His people. We'll look further into this in the chapter "Why Things Go Worse When We Pray."

It would be a tragedy to answer Yes to David's question, "Is it for nothing, then, that I have kept myself pure and have not committed sin?" Because the primary purpose of prayer is communication with God. It is *not* to get answers. If your primary purpose in prayer is to get answers, it won't be long before you will cease to pray, or your prayers will become simply a form, a routine. When your primary purpose in prayer is to communicate with God, then even God's apparent silence can lead you to seek Him more earnestly, and in the end draw you closer to Him.

Notice once again that when we speak of "getting answers," we are talking about receiving God's blessings, not getting a *response* from Him. Moses didn't get the *answer* he was after when he asked to be allowed into the Promised Land. But he received a *response*. Do you see the difference?

But there is a danger here that we need to guard against. While it is true that our primary purpose is not to get "things" from God, it is also true that we have been invited to ask Him to meet our needs—and even our wants. It would be a mistake to take prayer out of the realm of practical, daily life, and spiritualize it to the point that we exclude asking God for any of the blessings that He has promised to those who ask.

In his book *The Philippian Fragment*, Calvin Miller tells about a man who received a dramatic answer to prayer, when others, who prayed for the same thing, were denied. When the man was asked why *his* prayer was answered and what he learned from the experience, he gave some philosophical, high-sounding explanations. Then he concluded, "Oh yes—one more thing. It is always right to ask!"

Don't forget that ! It's always right to ask. We have been invited to ask. God *wants* us to ask. We may not always receive what we expect, but we are always welcome to ask.

We are invited to pray about everything (Philippians 4:6). We are invited to pray everywhere: "There is no time or place in which it is inappropriate to offer up a petition to God" (*Steps to Christ*, p. 99). We are invited to pray all the time: "Pray without ceasing" (1 Thessalonians 5:17).

If you read through the chapter on prayer in *Steps to Christ*, you will find a key word that is used repeatedly: *wants*. Have you ever had the idea that you were to pray only for your *needs*? No, God delights in having us bring our *wants* to Him as well. There is a classic paragraph on prayer in *Steps to Christ*. It begins like this: "Keep your *wants* . . . before God." Prayer for "wants" heads the list! The whole paragraph is so important that even though we looked at it in the previous chapter, I want to review it with you again:

Keep your *wants*, your joys, your sorrows, your cares, and your fears before God. You cannot burden Him; You cannot weary Him. He who numbers the hairs of your head is not indifferent to the *wants* of His children. "The Lord is very pitiful, and of tender mercy." . . . His heart of love is touched by our sorrows and even by our utterance of them. Take to Him everything that perplexes the mind. Nothing is too great for Him to bear, for He holds up worlds, He rules over all the affairs of the universe. Nothing that in any way concerns our peace is too small for Him to notice. There is no chapter in our ex-

perience too dark for Him to read; there is no perplexity
too difficult for Him to unravel. No calamity can befall
the least of His children, no anxiety harass the soul, no
joy cheer, no sincere prayer escape the lips, of which our
heavenly Father is unobservant, or in which He takes no
immediate interest. "He healeth the broken in heart, and
bindeth up their wounds." . . . The relations between God
and each soul are as distinct and full as though there
were not another soul upon earth to share His watchcare, not another soul for whom He gave His beloved Son
(*Steps to Christ*, p. 100).

Have you ever taken the time to *experience* this paragraph?
Notice God's advertising: No job too big, no job too small! And
in case we might miss something, we are given a list. "Keep
your *wants* (plural) . . . before God." What are your wants—
right now? Can you list three or four, or a dozen? "*Keep* your
wants . . . before God." Don't be satisfied with just telling Him
about them once or twice. *Keep* them before Him!

Keep your joys before God. What are you happy about right
now? Tell Him about that. Allow Him to share it with you.
Keep your sorrows before God. Do you have some? He's interested. Keep your cares before God. What is weighing you
down, right now? What are you concerned about? Place it
before God. Keep your fears before God. Wait a minute! If we
have faith in God, aren't we supposed to be free of fear?
Doesn't Revelation list fear along with other things that get
bad marks: "The fearful, and unbelieving, and the abominable,
. . . and all liars"? (Revelation 21:8).

"But Christians aren't supposed to be afraid," you say.

But *whether* you are supposed to be afraid, *are* you sometimes afraid? If so (and we all are), you are invited to keep
that before God too. When you find yourself among the fearful,
there's one right thing you can do about it. Keep your fears
before God. He knows how to bring peace.

So we are invited to ask—about everything, everywhere, all
the time! It pays to ask. We are invited to *keep* our requests
before God, because asking makes a difference. "It is a part of

God's plan to grant us, in answer to the prayer of faith, that which He would not bestow did we not thus ask" (*The Great Controversy*, p. 525).

When we ask for God's intervention in our lives, we are acknowledging our dependence upon Him. When we ask Him to come to our aid, we free Him, in His conflict with Satan, to work for us in ways He otherwise could not. No judge can rule in a case that has not been appealed to him.

Why do we pray? Because God is our Friend. That doesn't mean that we have exclusive rights to all of His blessings. Those who don't know Him will receive blessings at His hand, as He seeks to draw them to Himself. At times it may seem that they receive more than we do! But there are blessings that He gives only to His friends. In Proverbs 1:23 God says, "I would have poured out my heart to you" (NIV). The Revised Standard Version says, "I will pour out my thoughts to you." Smith and Goodspeed say, "Lo! I will open my mind to you, I will acquaint you with my thoughts."

When we commune with God in prayer, the sharing goes both ways. We can pour out our hearts to Him—and He will pour out His heart to us. And that blessing is available *only* for His close friends. Do you pour out your heart to just anybody, or are you particular? Do you choose to pour out your heart only to those you know really love you, those who are loyal to you and will respect your confidences?

Are you interested in coming close enough to the God of the universe that He will pour out His heart to you? Do you want to hear Him share His thoughts and plans? It's an awesome thought, isn't it?

We can afford to share the rain with the "unjust"! We can even accept it when the "unjust" get the rain while our own lives remain a desert. Because God is our friend, we will ask Him to send the rain; and we will often receive far more than if we had not asked. But the most important reason why we pray is to enter into the deepest fellowship and communion with Him, as He shares His thoughts with us and pours out His heart to us, the way He longs to do.

Chapter 4
Arguing With God

OK, let's acknowledge that the primary purpose in prayer is communion with God. Perhaps you have grown in your prayer life to the place where you are experiencing more and more of that yourself. But the time comes when you decide to bring a really *hard* request to the Lord. Of course, it's not hard for God. You're not worried about *that*. You know that nothing is impossible with Him. It's hard for *you*, because you're so anxious to receive it. We're talking about prayers of request in this chapter. Yours could be a request for temporal or spiritual blessings, but we're talking about the requests for desires that go deep—to the very core of our being.

This is the kind of prayer Job prayed while he was sitting on the edge of town, among the broken pottery and faithless friends. He had been looking for God so that he could talk to Him. He said, "If only I knew where to find him, . . . I would state my case before him and fill my mouth with arguments." *Job wanted to argue with God.*

It wasn't a matter of Job's trying to talk God into something that God was unwilling to do, that was against His will. Job had confidence in who God was and what he knew about God's character. He knew about God's willingness to bless and to give good things to those who walk with Him. Job didn't want to miss a single opportunity to receive what God was willing to give. If God was waiting for Job to seek Him wholeheartedly, Job was ready!

Sometimes God invites us to argue with Him! You can read

it in Isaiah: "Produce your cause, saith the Lord; bring forth your strong reasons, saith the King of Jacob" (Isaiah 41:21). All through the ages, God's people have come to Him with the requests nearest to their hearts and gathered their arguments to present along with those requests—reasons why God should respond to them. You may find many others, but here are fourteen of them that have been used by Bible pray-ers who were successful in prevailing with God.

Argument 1: Who God is

The Assyrians had come against Hezekiah with threatening letters that insulted God and His people. Hezekiah took the letter to the house of the Lord. Can you see him there, spreading out the letter on the floor of the temple? Now listen as he presents his arguments to God. He started with the argument of who God is:

> O Lord God of Israel, which dwellest between the cherubims, thou art the God, even thou alone, of all the kingdoms of the earth; thou has made heaven and earth (2 Kings 19:15).

God hardly needed a reminder of who He was—but Hezekiah may have needed to be reminded. In any case, that's where he started—with a statement about the power and majesty and position of God, the Ruler of the universe, the Lord of hosts.

Many Bible prayers begin that way. They start out reminding God of His power and majesty, acknowledging that He is a God above all gods, that He is the Creator, and that He has all power. It's not a bad place to start, is it?

We find the same approach used by Abraham. Abraham was arguing with God over the fate of Sodom, and he said, "Shall not the Judge of all the earth do right?" Abraham could present his case before God with confidence because he knew without a doubt who God was. God was the Judge of all the earth, and Abraham knew he could count on Him to deal righteously. That's why he was not afraid to press his case before Him.

Who God is becomes a mighty argument for us to bring before Him. Notice these words:

> Not one sincere prayer is lost. Amid the anthems of the celestial choir, God hears the cries of the weakest human being. We pour out our heart's desire in our closets, we breathe a prayer as we walk by the way, and our words reach the throne of the Monarch of the universe. They may be inaudible to any human ear, but they cannot die away into silence, nor can they be lost through the activities of business that are going on. Nothing can drown the soul's desire. It rises above the din of the street, above the confusion of the multitude, to the heavenly courts. *It is God* to whom we are speaking, and our prayer is heard (*Christ's Object Lessons*, p. 174, emphasis supplied).

It is God to whom we are speaking! And, more than that, He is our Father—and He is our Friend as well.

Suppose you had a special request to make, and you could take it to the president of the United States personally. Can you see yourself going in before him and saying, "Come on, grant this request; after all, you're the president"? But what if the president were also your father—and your friend? Why, the only way he would deny your request would be if he knew that to do so would cause you positive injury, or imperil the safety of the entire nation!

As if it is not enough that our God is the God of the entire universe, King of kings, and Lord of lords, He has added to His list of credentials the fact that He is our Father.

> In order to strengthen our confidence in God, Christ teaches us to address Him by a new name, a name entwined with the dearest associations of the human heart. He gives us the privilege of calling the infinite God our Father. This name, spoken to Him and of Him, is a sign of our love and trust toward Him, and a pledge of His regard and relationship to us. Spoken when asking

His favor or blessing, it is as music in His ears (*Christ's Object Lessons*, pp. 141, 142).

Next time you have an important request to make of God, remember this argument. Begin by reminding Him (and yourself) of who He is and what His relationship to you is. It's an argument that carries weight with Him!

Argument 2: For His own sake

It has been said that prayer is not a method for us to get our will done in heaven, but rather it is a method for God to get His will done on earth. "Prayer does not bring God down to us, but brings us up to Him" (*Steps to Christ*, p. 93). When we come to God in prayer, we are not praying for our sake alone, but for His sake as well. God says, "For mine own sake, even for mine own sake, will I do it: for how should my name be polluted? and I will not give my glory unto another" (Isaiah 48:11). "The Lord will not forsake his people for his great name's sake: because it hath pleased the Lord to make you his people" (1 Samuel 12:22). We even sing it in the twenty-third psalm: "He leadeth me in the paths of righteousness for his name's sake" (verse 3).

God's name, reputation, and glory are at stake when His people come to Him for help and deliverance. We can remind Him of this and ask Him to respond to our requests because of *His own* sake.

Argument 3: What will people think?

One of the best arguments we can bring as to why God should respond to our needs is His reputation and honor in the minds of other people. Moses used this argument during the travels from Egypt to the Promised Land:

Moses besought the Lord his God, and said, Lord, why doth thy wrath wax hot against thy people, which thou hast brought forth out of the land of Egypt with great power, and with a mighty hand? Wherefore should the Egyptians speak, and say, For mischief did he bring them out, to slay them in the mountains, and to consume them from the face of the earth? Turn from thy fierce wrath, and repent of this evil against thy people (Exodus 32:11, 12).

Notice again that Moses was not trying to convince God of something against His will. God was at work through His Spirit inspiring the prayers of Moses, because He delights in mercy. God was looking for any excuse to deliver His people. Unfortunately, they had been unfaithful to Him and had sinned against Him. They had taken themselves out of His hands, and the enemy was standing by, ready to call a foul if God should move in where He had not been invited. In Moses, God found the intercessor He had been searching for. Moses appealed the case to Him, and, once again, God was able to work in behalf of His people.

Joel said,

Spare thy people, O Lord, and give not thine heritage to reproach, that the heathen should rule over them: wherefore should they say among the people, Where is their God? (Joel 2:17).

When people are interested in exalting God's honor and reputation among those who don't know Him, and make this an argument in the requests they bring before Him, God pays special heed. "It is the glory of our God to give" (*The Desire of Ages*, p. 21). It is His glory. We glorify God before the universe when we bring our requests to Him, for His sake, for the sake of His reputation, that He may be glorified in the earth.

Argument 4: Saying Yes is fun for God!
God delights to answer us when we bring Him our requests. It is His pleasure to bring pleasure and joy to His people. Through Jeremiah God says, "I will rejoice over them to do them good." "It shall be to me a name of joy, a praise and an honour before all the nations of the earth, which shall hear all

the good that I do unto them" (Jeremiah 32:41; 33:9). "God delights to give" (*Christ's Object Lessons*, p. 141).

How's this for an argument to bring with our requests before the Lord? Can we pray, "Father, it will be so much fun for You to grant this request"? Is that going too far?

Remember when you were small and you tried to convince your parents to do something for you? If you knew that a particular thing was fun for them, you had a better chance of getting a positive response, didn't you? If your Dad loved to go camping, and you asked him to take you on a camping trip, you were halfway there before you even started!

Since God delights to give, we are not asking Him to do something contrary to His nature. We are inviting Him to do something that brings Him great joy. How interesting that He would let us know about this aspect of His character so that we can come with greater confidence when we bring our requests to Him.

Argument 5: The argument of the cross

One of the greatest reasons why we can go to God with our requests is the cross of Christ. "He that spared not his own Son, but delivered him up for us all, how shall he not with him also freely give us all things?" (Romans 8:32). It is the righteousness of Christ, made available to us through His sacrifice on the cross, that enables us to approach God's throne with confidence.

Daniel used this argument in asking God to hear and respond to his prayer. He said, "O my God, incline thine ear, and hear; open thine eyes, and behold our desolations, and the city which is called by thy name: for we do not present our supplications before thee for our righteousness, but for thy great mercies" (Daniel 9:18). We have no righteousness of our own to present as an argument for why God should answer our prayers. But in His mercy He has given His Son to become our righteousness, and because of the righteousness of Christ, we can come to Him.

One of the greatest reasons we do not get answers to our prayers is that we go to God presenting our own goodness, our own track record, as a reason for Him to hear us. Have you ever heard someone pray, "Please help this person. Remember how faithful they have been to you. Remember all their years of service in your work." The Jewish leaders said that about the centurion. "He deserves Your help because he has built us a synagogue." But the centurion said of himself, "I am not worthy" (see Luke 7:2-6).

The best we can do, when we come before the throne of God, is to join the songwriter in saying,

> Nothing in my hand I bring,
> Simply to Thy cross I cling.

"The death of Christ was an argument in man's behalf that could not be overthrown" (*The Great Controversy*, p. 502).

Argument 6: But you promised!

Remember when your children were small (or when you were small!), and they would come and ask you to do such and such a thing. While you were considering the matter, they would say, "But you *promised*!" And if you had promised, you knew right then that you'd "had it," as soon as they presented that argument!

God is willing for us to use this as an argument when we bring our requests to Him. "Whereby are given unto us exceeding great and precious promises: that by these ye might be partakers of the divine nature, having escaped the corruption that is in the world through lust" (2 Peter 1:4).

We are assured, "Blessed be the Lord, that hath given rest unto his people Israel, according to all that he promised: there hath not failed one word of all his good promise, which he promised by the hand of Moses his servant" (1 Kings 8:56).

"God stands back of every promise He has made." "The honor of His throne is staked for the fulfillment of His Word unto us" (*Christ's Object Lessons*, pp. 147, 148).

We will be taking a longer look at claiming Bible promises in the chapter called "Prayer and Faith." Not every promise in the Word of God is for you, at this time, under these circumstances.

You may not know when to claim His promise, "I will deliver thee, and thou shalt glorify me," and when to claim His promise, "Be thou faithful unto death, and I will give thee a crown of life" (Psalm 50:15; Revelation 2:10). Some promises are conditional, and we must have wisdom from above to know when these promises apply to our particular situation.

But spiritual promises are always available. God may not give us the temporal blessings we desire—even to the preserving of life itself. Many of those who lived the closest to Him died martyrs' deaths. But He has always provided for our spiritual needs, and for these we can bring His promise and know that He hears and will respond as He promised.

Sometimes we do not understand His thoughts and promises toward us, yet His word is nonetheless sure of reaching its fulfillment:

> As the heavens are higher than the earth, so are my ways higher than your ways and my thoughts than your thoughts. As the rain and the snow come down from heaven, and do not return to it without watering the earth and making it bud and flourish, so that it yields seed for the sower and bread for the eater, so is my word that goes out from my mouth: It will not return to me empty, but will accomplish what I desire and achieve the purpose for which I sent it (Isaiah 55:9-11, NIV).

When we present to God His promises, we have a sure guarantee: Either He will send us that which we are expecting from Him, or, if we have misunderstood His purpose because His thoughts and ways are so much higher than ours, He will send us something better!

Argument 7: "You've done it for others"

> It is no secret what God can do.
> What He's done for others, He'll do for you.
> With arms wide open, He'll pardon you.
> It is no secret what God can do.

David brings this same argument to the Lord: "Our fathers trusted in thee: they trusted, and thou didst deliver them. They cried unto thee, and were delivered: they trusted in thee, and were not confounded" (Psalm 22:4).

In legal circles, it's good news if the attorney is able to discover a case that sets the precedent for the decision he is hoping to get for his client. If no precedent has been set, it's likely to be a long, hard winter! But when the lawyer can present before the judge the fact that in the case of Smith vs. Jones, back at such and such a time, a similar ruling was made, it gives an advantage. In the same way, we can remind God of what He has done for others, as an argument of why He is free to work in like manner for us.

> The records of sacred history are written, not merely that we may read and wonder, but that the same faith which wrought in God's servants of old may work in us. In no less marked manner will the Lord work now, wherever there are hearts of faith to be channels of His power (*Prophets and Kings*, p. 175).

No wonder Jesus was surprised at the faith of the leper who first came to Him. Naaman had been healed, but that was years before. Jesus had healed all manner of disease, but so far, no lepers had been healed. Ellen White says that the lepers feared to come to Jesus, because "they dared not expect Jesus to do for them what He had never done for any man" (*The Desire of Ages*, p. 263). But after one leper reached out in faith and was healed, many lepers came to receive a like blessing—on one occasion even ten at a time!

So we *can* bring our requests to God, even if we are asking Him to do for us what He has "never done for any man." But how much more boldly we can come, bringing the argument of what He *has done* for others.

Argument 8: What He has done for us in the past

Do you ever feel like you shouldn't keep asking God over and over for the same blessings? Are you ever afraid that you've used up your turns, and now He won't be able to help you again? Here's an interesting comment: "If you abide in Him, the fact that you receive a rich gift today insures the reception of a richer gift tomorrow" (*The Desire of Ages*, p. 148). Add to that this one: God "is well pleased when we urge past mercies and blessings as a reason why He should bestow on us greater blessings" (*The Ministry of Healing*, p. 513).

Moses instructed the Israelites how to approach the Lord in time of need. He told them to go to the tabernacle with a gift for the priest. Then he said, "Thou shalt speak and say before the Lord thy God" (Deuteronomy 26:5). What does he tell them to speak? He tells them to list the times when God has delivered them in the past. Deuteronomy 8:2 says the same thing: "Thou shalt remember all the way which the Lord thy God led thee these forty years in the wilderness, to humble thee, and to prove thee, to know what was in thine heart, whether thou wouldest keep his commandments, or no."

What is Ellen White's classic sentence? "We have nothing to fear for the future" except what? "Except as we shall forget the way the Lord has led us" (*Testimonies to Ministers*, p. 31). As we remember His dealings with us in the past, we are encouraged to trust Him for today.

Argument 9: He has invited us to ask!

We do not come before the Lord on our own initiative. We do not burst into His presence without an appointment. He has issued the invitation. We are invited to ask:

> Ask, and it shall be given you; seek, and ye shall find; knock, and it shall be opened unto you: for every one that asketh receiveth; and he that seeketh findeth; and to him that knocketh it shall be opened (Matthew 7:7, 8).

> This is the confidence that we have in him, that, if we ask any thing according to his will, he heareth us: and if we know that he hear us, whatsoever we ask, we know that we have the petitions that we desired of him (1 John 5:14, 15).

Let's add to that two short sentences from the book *Mount of Blessing:* "The asking, makes it manifest that you realize your necessity; and if you ask in faith, you will receive." "Your heavenly Father knows that you have need of all these things, and you are invited to ask Him concerning them" (pp. 130, 133).

Does it make a difference, when you approach an earthly friend for a favor, if he has already made you an offer of assistance? Suppose your car breaks down and you have to call someone to help you out. Whom do you call? Of course, the person who has already said, "If you need anything, just give me a call." If he or she seemed to be sincere in that offer, it's easier to call him, isn't it?

When we bring our requests to God, we can say, "God, I'm here because You invited me. You *said* to come to You in time of need. So here I am." We can have confidence in His willingness to bless, because He has invited us to seek Him for His blessings.

Argument 10: Our great need

"Our great need is itself an argument, and pleads most eloquently in our behalf" (*Steps to Christ*, p. 95).

Jonah cried unto God from the inside of a whale! Notice his prayer: "I cried *by reason of mine affliction* unto the Lord, and he heard me" (Jonah 2:2, emphasis supplied). Jonah couldn't present any better reason for God to deliver him than the reason of his affliction. He had a great need, and God responded to that need.

The Old Testament tells us of a most unusual battle between the Israelite choir and the enemy: "O our God, wilt thou not judge them? for we have no might against this great company that cometh against us; neither know we what to do: but our eyes are upon thee" (2 Chronicles 20:12). They had an urgent need, and realized their own inability to defend themselves, and, as a result, God brought a mighty deliverance for them.

It is when you come to the end of your own resources and cry out for help from above that God is free to move in with

His power. His heart of love is touched when He sees our help-lessness, and so we can bring to Him our need as one of the reasons why He should come to our aid.

Argument 11: "I'm not asking this for myself"

Prayers for others give a special tug on God's heartstrings. He is in sympathy with our needs for ourselves, but when we come to Him bringing the needs of those around us, He is especially mindful, for in so doing we have entered into His spirit of ministry for others.

Jesus told a parable about a man seeking bread for a friend at midnight (Luke 11:5-8). This parable brings the assurance that God will respond to our prayers for the needs of others. "Never will one be told, I cannot help you. Those who beg at midnight for loaves to feed the hungry will be successful" (*Christ's Object Lessons*, p. 148). Do you want a carte blanche? Here it is: *Never* does one seek the bread of life to share with hungry souls, and receive a denial. Success is guaranteed. *You will receive the help you seek.*

Now it would be possible, I suppose, to use prayer for others as an excuse for getting things for one's self. Even prayers for others can at times be selfish. One time I heard the young people singing, "Give me gas for my Mercedes. Keep me haul-ing Dorcas ladies"! That was pretty transparent! And God is not to be fooled by the games we may play.

But anytime we pray for others because we sincerely desire God's blessing for them, our requests will be honored.

Argument 12: Nowhere else to go

When Jesus had finished His sermon in John 6, explaining the spiritual nature of His kingdom and the fellowship with Him that He was offering, the crowds that had been following Him disappeared. They had been attracted by the loaves and the fishes—but the offer of the Bread of Life was unappealing to their unconverted hearts.

Jesus turned to His disciples and asked, "Are you going away too?"

They replied, "Lord, to whom shall we go?" (verse 68).

It almost sounds as if they would have left, too, had there been anyplace for them to go. But they were right. When it comes to meeting the deepest needs of the soul, we have no alternative. There *is* nowhere else to go. David said, "Whom have I in heaven but thee? and there is none upon earth that I desire beside thee" (Psalm 73:25). And Peter added, "Neither is there salvation in any other: for there is none other name under heaven given among men, whereby we must be saved" (Acts 4:12). "We have nothing to recommend us to God: but the plea that we may urge now and ever is our utterly helpless condition that makes His redeeming power a necessity" (*The Desire of Ages*, p. 317).

Suppose you need some oil for your car. There are any number of places you can go. If you don't get waited on quickly enough at the first gas station, or if you don't like their price, you can leave. There's no need to be persistent—no need to keep urging your case.

But suppose your child has contracted a rare disease, and only one doctor in the whole world has successfully treated such cases. You don't take No for an answer. You move heaven and earth to get your child under the care of that physician. What makes the difference? You have nowhere else to turn!

There is only one physician who can treat the needs of the soul: the Great Physician. As we come into His presence, seeking His healing and help, we can use this as an argument: "Lord, to whom shall we go? thou hast the words of eternal life."

Argument 13: I won't let you go

This is the "Jacob argument." Jacob had reached the end of his own resources, and he was in desperate need. As soon as he discovered that he was fighting with Jesus, he hung on for his very life. He said, "I won't let you go until you bless me" (see Genesis 32:26).

Have you ever persisted in prayer to God, and finally said, "Are you getting tired of hearing me ask you this same thing over and over?" *I hope so!* Have you ever dared to use the

Jacob argument, and pray, "I will not let you go until you bless me"?

We are invited to persist in prayer. God is pleased when we continue to press our case before Him until He responds to our cries for help. In fact, the very persistence comes from Him in the first place! Speaking first of the Syrophoenician woman, Ellen White said:

> It was Christ Himself who put into that mother's heart the persistence which would not be repulsed. It was Christ who gave the pleading widow courage and determination before the judge. It was Christ who, centuries before, in the mysterious conflict by the Jabbok, had inspired Jacob with the same preserving faith. And the confidence which He Himself had implanted, He did not fail to reward (*Christ's Object Lessons*, p. 175).

Argument 14: The James argument

This final argument that we can give to God is actually one He gives to us, which we can then turn around and apply back to Him. James said:

> What doth it profit, my brethren, though a man say he hath faith, and have not works? can faith save him? If a brother or sister be naked, and destitute of daily food, and one of you say unto them, Depart in peace, be ye warmed and filled; notwithstanding ye give them not those things which are needful to the body; what doth it profit? Even so faith, if it hath not works, is dead, being alone (James 2:14-17).

Ellen White said that "words are of no value unless they are accompanied with appropriate deeds" (*Christ's Object Lessons*, p. 272).

Well, you say, what does that have to do with prayer? Just this: it is *God* who says, Put your money where your mouth is. Isn't that what He's saying here? Don't just say the words. Words alone are not enough. Words won't keep you warm in the winter or clothe the naked or feed the hungry. So put your money where your mouth is.

If God asks us to do this, why wouldn't He do the same? God is not simply speaking empty words when He gives us His promises, inviting us to come to Him, bringing our needs. He is willing to match His words with all the resources of heaven.

You can come to God with the James argument and remind Him that unless He follows *His* words with actions, the words aren't worth much.

"Isn't that getting a little bold with God?" you say. Just remember where the argument came from—it came from the Word of God!

One time a group of us were praying for a little boy who was dying. The family was facing a major crisis. We were gathered in the home, and one of the godly sisters began praying for their need. I can still remember her words: "God, we're going to hold You to this one." I think God was pleased!

Remember—we do not serve a God who is looking for any excuse He can find to *keep* from helping us in our times of need. No, He's looking for any excuse to bring us His deliverance. Because of our humanity, we may not know how to pray as we ought. We may ask for all the wrong things. But when we come to Him, not one prayer is lost. We may not receive the *exact* response we expect—but we will receive a response. Those who ask, receive.

In your times of crisis, when you feel your need of God so desperately that you go through every argument in the book, and then start all over again—just remember: You are not seeking in vain. You are asking for a purpose. God *will* respond to your search for Him, and He will bring you the help that best meets your need.

Chapter 5
Intercessory Prayer

One day a woman went to visit the pastor of her church. She said, "I am concerned for my husband. He has never been converted. Would you please pray for him?"

The pastor replied, "I will pray for your husband for one hour every day, if you will pray for your husband for one hour every day."

After considering the matter briefly, the woman said, "Never mind." And she left the office.

What is your reaction to this woman? Do you think, Well, that pastor sure knew how to smoke her out of the woods? Obviously she wasn't that concerned about her husband, after all? Or do you think this woman was just being honest, admitting that she wouldn't be able to keep up her end of the bargain?

What would you do if someone made a similar offer to you? Would you go home and faithfully pray for your friend or relative for one hour every day? Would you be able to do it? Have you ever prayed for an entire hour for just one person? Could you do it again tomorrow—and the day after that, and the day after that?

Perhaps some of us would have agreed to the arrangement and struggled through ten or fifteen minutes the first day, five minutes the second day, and after that hoped that the pastor would follow through even though we didn't!

In a church that I pastored several years ago, we decided to have a series on the subject of prayer during our Wednesday night meetings. It didn't take long for the discussions to center around one key question: What difference does prayer make? If you pray for someone, and he knows you are praying for him, perhaps that would have some psychological benefit. But what if you pray for someone who doesn't know you are praying for him? Does that help? How could it? Why would it? After all, is it fair for God to bless this person here, who has someone praying for him, and withhold a blessing from that person over there, just because he doesn't have anyone praying for him?

After twisting our brains all out of shape for some time, someone finally suggested, "Why don't we try it and find out? Let's choose an impossible case, and pray for that person, both in the group on Wednesday nights and privately in our homes. Let's see what happens."

I had visited an "impossible" case that very day. There was a family in the community who had been members of the church years before. In fact, they had even been to the mission field. But someone did them wrong, and they felt bitter, disillusioned, and angry. They hated the church. They hated preachers. As I left their home that afternoon, they shouted, "And don't pray for us!"

But that was one thing over which they had no control!

So I mentioned the names of these people to the congregation. Everyone nodded in agreement. The family was well-known in the community. It was truly an impossible case. We decided to make that family our test case. We would pray for them specifically in our private prayers at home all through the week.

That first week their house burned down! The news came out in the local paper. When we gathered for prayer meeting the following Wednesday I asked my congregation, "What are you people praying for, anyway?"

We continued praying. The second week, the newspaper reported that a valuable piece of equipment that this family used in their business had been stolen. And so it went. One thing after another went wrong for them. We just kept on praying and watching.

The last Sabbath of that month, the entire family walked into church. Heads turned—and then quickly turned back again, and word flew from one person to another, "They're here!" After church, one by one the people came to me and said, "We ought to do more praying!"

Why does prayer make a difference?

The Lord is the Judge—the righteous Judge of the universe. It's an analogy that is found often in Scripture. Paul said:

> There is laid up for me a crown of righteousness, which the Lord, the righteous judge, shall give me at that day: and not to me only, but unto all them also that love his appearing (2 Timothy 4:8).

Another familiar verse is 1 John 2:1: "My little children, these things write I unto you, that ye sin not. And if any man sin, we have an advocate with the Father, Jesus Christ the righteous."

What is an advocate? These are some of the other words that mean the same thing: lawyer, attorney, intercessor, mediator. Isaiah 53:12 talks about Jesus as Intercessor for the transgressors. Romans 8:34 says that Christ is at the right hand of God making intercession for us. Hebrews 7:25 says that "he ever liveth to make intercession for" us. First Timothy 2:5, 6 speaks of Jesus as the Mediator between God and man. These words describe the role of Jesus and the Father in their relationship to us.

That is good Bible evidence as to why God can do things when we pray, that He can't do when we don't pray. Any judge, mediator, or intercessor, any attorney or lawyer, would overstep his bounds if he took on the defense of a case that had not been appealed to him. This is particularly true when a prosecution is involved. Prosecutors watch like hawks for any opportunity to declare a mistrial. If an attorney or judge should undertake to defend a case that had not been appealed to him, you can be sure the prosecutor would make the most of it! So it is with God the Father and Jesus and even the Holy

Spirit, who intercedes for us with groanings which cannot be uttered. Although they are anxious to work in our behalf, there are certain limitations. When we pray for ourselves or for others and appeal a case to Them, They are free to work in a way that otherwise would not be allowed.

This is one of the reasons, in terms of the great controversy, why prayer makes a difference. But the next thing we need to understand is what kind of difference prayer *can* make—and what kind of difference prayer can *not* make.

Let's try another parable!

Walking to the Promised Land

Let's say that one day you are walking from San Francisco to Pacific Union College—the "Promised Land"! I come driving along in my car, pull over beside you, and ask, "Where are you going?"

"I'm going to Pacific Union College—the Promised Land," you say.

"That's where I'm going," I reply. "Get in, and I'll take you there."

Now you will arrive at PUC a lot faster. You will get fewer blisters along the way and have an easier trip. But you *were* going to get there anyway.

Now let's reverse it with an opposite parable.

Walking to Las Vegas

One day you are walking from San Francisco to Las Vegas—the other place! I come driving along in my car, pull over beside you, and ask, "Where are you going?"

You say, "I'm going to Las Vegas—the other place!"

"That's where I'm going too," I say. "Get in, and I'll take you there."

Now you will arrive at Las Vegas a lot faster. You will get fewer blisters along the way—although you will get *more* blisters when you get there! But you were going there anyway.

Sometimes when I have used this parable, people try to reverse it and confuse it and complicate it. They say, "What if you come along and offer me a ride to PUC, and I was going to Las Vegas?" or, "What if you offer me a ride to Las Vegas, and I was going to PUC?" Or, "What if I *think* I'm going to PUC, but really I'm headed for Las Vegas?" Or, "What if you *think* you are going to take me to PUC, but really you take me to Las Vegas?" And so on and on! But in terms of eternal salvation, we know that God will never make one person's eternal salvation based on what someone else does or doesn't do. Jesus is the Light that lighteth every one who comes into the world (see John 1:9).

According to Scripture, God is a God of love, and according to Scripture, He is responsible for you being born into this world. It wasn't the devil, and it wasn't your parents. It was God. If those two ideas are true—that God is a God of love who is responsible for our being born—then He would have to give every person an adequate chance for something better.

The only choice that can determine whether you are going to "PUC" or "Las Vegas" is your own choice. No one else can decide that for you. When it comes to your eternal salvation, you are guaranteed an adequate chance to accept eternal life. This doesn't mean that everyone has an equal chance. Those who have been raised in a Christian environment and know much of the things of God and heaven certainly have an advantage over those in the darkness of heathenism who never heard the name of Jesus. But everyone, at some time during his or her lifetime, will have an adequate opportunity to choose God.

In the judgment, no one will be able to legitimately point to another person and say, "He's the reason why I'm not going to be saved." Each will understand that he decided his destiny for himself.

However, the fact that we do not hold the salvation of others in our hands does not mean that God cannot use our hands to extend the offer of salvation to them. We can be channels of His working; we can be the means He uses to reach those who are willing to be reached. So we *can* have a part in someone else's salvation. We can hasten the process. We can help them get there more quickly! We can save them many trials and heartaches and bruises along the way. We can bring them the peace of God years earlier than would otherwise be possible.

We'll look at this more in the chapter called "Prayer and Witness." But for now, let's nail down just this much: Our prayers can be a part of the process of hastening God's work in the lives of those around us.

Lend me three loaves

One of the most beautiful passages of Scripture on the subject of intercessory prayer is found in Luke 11:5-8. Let's take the time to read it carefully:

> He said unto them, Which of you shall have a friend, and shall go unto him at midnight, and say unto him, Friend, lend me three loaves; for a friend of mine in his journey is come to me, and I have nothing to set before him? And he from within shall answer and say, Trouble me not: the door is now shut, and my children are with me in bed; I cannot rise and give thee. I say unto you, Though he will not rise and give him, because he is his friend, yet because of his importunity he will rise and give him as many as he needeth.

Then follows Jesus' famous promise, "Ask, and it shall be given you; seek, and ye shall find," and so forth (verse 9). It was given in the context of this parable about praying for others.

Put yourself in the picture. You have a friend who has been traveling across the country. He comes to your house late at night, and he's hungry. But you have nothing to offer him. Your cupboard is bare. Your pantry is empty. Maybe you were planning to go grocery shopping tomorrow, but he's hungry now. It's midnight, and the 7-Eleven closed an hour ago. What are you going to do?

First, the question is *not* whether your friend will starve to death. The question is whether he will go to bed hungry. His *life* is not in your hands, but his *comfort* is.

So you hurry over to the pastor's house and knock on the

door. The pastor and his family are asleep. The pastor is quite unhappy that you have awakened him in the middle of the night. Apparently he doesn't even come to the front door. He just opens the bedroom window and calls out from upstairs, "Don't bother me. We're in bed asleep. The door is shut. Come back tomorrow."

But you stay right there. You say, "I have a friend who has come to me for help, and I have nothing to give him. You've *got* to help." And you persist in your appeals.

Do you think you could do that? Would you be intimidated by the fact that you were causing inconvenience to someone else? Or would you be so intent on getting something for your friend who is in need that you would persist, in spite of the apparent dismissal?

Notice the three factors that enable you to continue pleading, even in the face of obstacles. First, you have a friend who is in need. You're not asking this for yourself, but for someone else. That fact adds extra courage that would otherwise be missing. Second, the one upon whose door you are knocking has what is needed. You know ahead of time that you will be able to get what you need for your friend from this source. In spite of the lateness of the hour and the untimeliness of the request, the response is not, "I don't have any bread either; go home and go to bed," but rather, "Don't bother me."

And finally, you and the pastor are already friends! He may not seem too friendly right now—but sometimes the lack of politeness can be an indication of friendship, can't it? If you were some stranger, the pastor might be quicker to put his best foot forward—to play his official role. But since it's just you, he trusts your friendship enough to say, "Don't bother me!" Have you ever had it happen that way?

But you *are* friends, not only with the one *for* whom you seek the three loaves—but also with the one *from* whom you seek them. Notice how the midnight petitioner began his request: *"Friend,* lend me three loaves." There is an already established relationship here, which the one making the request is not afraid to depend upon.

Have you ever seen the little motto "The test of friendship

is not how you handle each other's words, but how you handle each other's silence"? Friends don't have to chatter constantly to know they are friends. They can be comfortable together, even in silence. Is that true of your friendship with God? Are you comfortable with His silence? Do you know Him well enough for that?

We are told that Jesus told this parable by way of contrast, not comparison. God is willing to give and delights in responding to our requests. But there are times when He is silent for a time in order to test the genuineness of our desires, of our trust in Him. Andrew Murray quotes from this parable in his book on intercessory prayer, and suggests that perhaps the reason Jesus used contrast to make His point was that He couldn't find anyone in real life whom He could use by way of comparison! Perhaps so. But because of the first three facts, the one seeking loaves at midnight comes to a definite conclusion. He says, I have a friend in need; you have what this friend and I need; you and I are friends as well, and so I'm not leaving. I'm staying here until you produce the goods!

Do you have a friend in need? Do you realize your own helplessness to meet his need? But do you know another Friend who has all power and all the resources of heaven and earth at His command? The assurance of Jesus' story is that you *can* go to your heavenly Friend and be assured of the help that the situation requires. The parable ends on a triumphant note: The one who has sought for help at midnight was given as much help as he needed.

"Never will one be told, I cannot help you. Those who beg at midnight for loaves to feed the hungry souls will be successful" (*Christ's Object Lessons*, p. 148).

Andrew Murray writes in his book *The Ministry of Intercession*:

If we will but believe in God and His faithfulness, intercession will become to us the very first thing we take refuge in when we seek blessing for others; and the very last thing for which we cannot find time.

Chapter 6
Conditions to Answered Prayer

This is the scary chapter! Only one chapter in this book is worse, and that's the chapter right after this one! In this chapter we will examine the conditions to answered prayer, and in the next chapter we will focus on the one condition that often causes the greatest anxiety: *No known sin in the life.* So if you are too nervous to wait, go ahead to the next chapter, and then come back here after you finish it to get the rest of the story!

Perhaps you have heard it said, "Things that are too good to be true usually are." A lot of things look great on the surface, but when you read the small print, you discover that they are not such a bargain, after all. As a Christian, you are encouraged to pray, to bring your needs to God, to ask whatever you will, and you are assured that it will be done. Sooner or later, though, you will have to face the small print. Sooner or later you must look at the condition for answered prayer. This may frighten you, but it is essential to a successful prayer life.

One reason why it is so important to understand the conditions to answered prayer is that prayer is not an end in itself. It is not "good works" or a way to gain extra merit. While we are told that much prayer is vital if it's the right kind (2 Thessalonians 5:17), we are also told that much prayer is worthless if it's the wrong kind (Matthew 6:7).

So let's brave the consequences and spend a few moments studying the conditions for effective prayer.

Realize your need

The first condition to answered prayer is to have a need, and to realize that you have a need. If you have no need of God, no need of His help, why should you ask for it in the first place? Also, if you have a need but are not aware of it, you won't be motivated to go for help. That seems logical, doesn't it?

One family tried to convince their father to go to the doctor for help. It was very apparent to *them* that he was in need, but *he* thought he was doing just fine. After much arguing and urging they finally got him into the doctor's office, but he refused to cooperate with the doctor, insisting that he didn't need anything.

After the examination the doctor told the family members, "Yes, your father is in need of medical attention, but it looks like he's going to have to get worse before we can help him."

It still haunts me to remember a hospital visit I had several years ago with a man who thought he had a stomachache and said he would be as good as new in just a few days. The family asked me to visit him, and it became apparent in just a short time that no one had told him that he was going to die that night. He had a need, but he didn't know about it.

Millions of people are in desperate spiritual need, but they are unaware of the fact, so they don't seek God for help. Many people *in the church* are in the same dilemma. It's the major problem of the church. It's called Laodicea:

> Because thou sayest, I am rich, and increased with goods, and have need of nothing; and knowest not that thou art wretched, and miserable, and poor, and blind, and naked (Revelation 3:17).

Perhaps you heard about the rare medical condition that makes the victim unable to feel pain. I was a youngster the first time I heard about that, and it seemed like such a wonderful possibility! No more need to worry when it was time to get another shot or go see the dentist. Next time I fell off of my bicycle—no big deal! In fact, what a wonderful guarantee never again to worry about a spanking!

But then I learned a little more and began to realize what a blessing pain can be. People who have this condition can be slicing tomatoes and cut off the end of a finger! They can bleed to death from some gaping wound and never even notice that they were injured. God says:

> I will pour water upon him that is thirsty, and floods upon the dry ground: I will pour my spirit upon thy seed, and my blessing upon thine offspring (Isaiah 44:3).

You have to be thirsty in order to appreciate or desire water. The ground has to be dry in order to absorb the rain.

How do you get thirsty? Salt makes you thirsty, and we're told that salt represents the righteousness of Christ. Being in the sun makes you thirsty. When Jesus, the Sun of righteousness, is uplifted, He will make you want to drink at the fountain of life. Exercise makes you thirsty. What is exercise in the Christian life? Service, outreach, and working for others. God has provided many avenues to make us aware of our need, so we will be ready to accept the help that only He can bring.

Ask for help

This may seem rather elementary, but one of the conditions to answered prayer is that we pray in the first place! God loves to respond to those who ask, but He's not pushy about it. He doesn't crowd His blessings onto anyone, but He is very pleased when we ask Him for help.

One Christmas my son decided he wanted a particular bicycle. There was just one problem: That bicycle was not available in any store. No one was selling a bicycle with the special features he wanted.

I drove all over Los Angeles hunting for parts to that bicycle, and managed to pick up a wheel here, a brake there, a handlebar somewhere else. I worked in the garage early and late. Christmas morning I was still hiding in the garage when he came out to find his new bicycle. It's a good thing he liked it! It would have been a long, hard winter if he hadn't!

Any parent knows the fun of giving a child something that he has especially asked to receive. Is God any different? He tells us in so many words, "Ask, and it shall be given you; seek, and ye shall find; knock, and it shall be opened unto you" (Luke 11:9).

Of course, God knows our needs before we ask, so why ask? The first reason is that He told us to, but there are good reasons for asking.

Since prayer is the vital link in the communication between God and man, it is when we pray and He answers that we know He is at work in our lives, and that we are not just victims of fate or coincidence.

Notice Jesus' prayer at the tomb of Lazarus:

> Jesus lifted up his eyes, and said, Father, I thank thee that thou hast heard me. And I knew that thou hearest me always: but because of the people which stand by I said it, that they may believe that thou hast sent me (John 11:41, 42).

There was more at stake in the raising of Lazarus than simply getting Lazarus back to life again. Jesus wanted to show the people a mighty evidence of His connection with God—His relationship with His Father in heaven. By asking God to raise Lazarus in the hearing of all the people, Jesus made it obvious that God was at work in His life and that God's Son was not operating independently.

The same concept is presented in John 13:19. Jesus told His disciples what would come to pass, explaining that "I am telling you now before it happens, so that when it does happen you will believe" (NIV).

When we ask in prayer for the blessing of God, He is then free to pour out His blessings without the danger that we will assume we brought the blessing on ourselves. Asking prevents our taking the credit for the work of God in our lives.

Asking also reminds us of our dependent condition, that we are His children. When we come into His presence and present our requests, we are reminded who is in control in our lives.

Have you ever had a highway patrolman stop you and ask to see your driver's license? The officer may phrase his command as a question, but he's not really *asking* if he can see your driver's license. He's just phrasing his demand in a polite way! People who are in a position of authority don't ask. They tell!

But when we bring our petitions before the throne of God, we are asking. We are dependent upon Him because He is the Creator, and we are only creatures. He is God, and we are not. He has all power, and we are helpless. So we ask. It is one of the prerequisites for receiving special blessing from Him.

No cherished sin

Here's the big one! We will mention it only briefly here, because we will spend a chapter on it all by itself. Psalm 66:18 says it: "If I regard iniquity in my heart, the Lord will not hear me." In *Steps to Christ* we read:

> If we regard iniquity in our hearts, if we cling to any known sin, the Lord will not hear us; but the prayer of the penitent, contrite soul is always accepted. When all known wrongs are righted, we may believe that God will answer our petitions. Our own merit will never commend us to the favor of God; it is the worthiness of Jesus that will save us, His blood that will cleanse us; yet we have a work to do in complying with the conditions of acceptance (p. 95).

Faith in God

Here is one that you would expect to show up on the list: Faith. Well, of course! The classic text is Hebrews 11:6: "He that cometh to God must believe that he is, and that he is a rewarder of them that diligently seek him." It's interesting the way it is worded. God is a rewarder of them that diligently seek *Him*. Not those who seek merely His blessings, but those who seek *Him*, are the ones who find their reward. For *He* is the reward.

Notice that there are two parts to this belief, or faith. First, we must believe that He is, and second, we must believe that

He rewards those who seek Him—and *He* is the reward. If this is true, then true faith is more interested in seeking the Giver than in seeking the gifts. The minute I become more concerned with the gifts than with the Giver, the way is obstructed for me to experience His gifts. That's an interesting principle.

Ellen White quotes this passage from Hebrews 11, and then comments:

> The assurance is broad and unlimited, and He is faithful who has promised. When we do not receive the very things we ask for, at the time we ask, we are still to believe that the Lord hears and that He will answer our prayers. We are so erring and shortsighted that we sometimes ask for things that would not be a blessing to us, and our heavenly Father in love answers our prayers by giving us that which will be for our highest good—that which we ourselves would desire if with vision divinely enlightened we could see all things as they really are. When our prayers seem not to be answered, we are to cling to the promise; for the time of answering will surely come, and we shall receive the blessing we need most. But to claim that prayer will always be answered in the very way and for the particular thing that we desire, is presumption. God is too wise to err, and too good to withhold any good thing from them that walk uprightly. Then do not fear to trust Him, even though you do not see the immediate answer to your prayers. Rely upon His sure promise, "Ask, and it shall be given you" (*Steps to Christ,* p. 96).

So faith involves more than just believing that God will answer our prayers in the exact way that we expect Him to work. Our faith is in *Him*, not in a specific answer or response from Him. We can be certain of a response—but we cannot dictate what His response will be.

Faith is not what we've sometimes been led to think. It is not believing that we are going to get what we ask from God. Faith is believing that He hears and answers, whether or not we get what we ask for. Faith is trusting that He knows what is best and will surely give us what is best. We will spend a separate chapter on this subject a little later on.

Perseverance

A story appeared in *Insight* magazine several years ago, titled something like "Sherry Asked Once." The story was about a girl who had lost her purse, and she and her friends prayed and asked God to find it for her. After spending more time looking, and being unable to locate the purse, one of her friends said, "Shouldn't we pray again?"

"Why?" she replied. "We already asked God about it. Do you think He didn't hear? Do you think He is deaf? Why would we need to ask Him again?"

So she didn't ask again, much to the uneasiness of her friends. She simply went her way, leaving the matter in the Lord's hands. Several weeks later the purse was returned to her intact.

That story reminds me of the experience of Elijah on Mount Carmel. The prophets of Baal had spent the entire day begging, pleading, and dancing around their altar. Elijah said to them, "Cry louder! Maybe your god is asleep. Maybe he is talking to someone else, and not paying attention. Maybe he's on a journey."

When Elijah's turn came, after he had prepared his altar, what did he do? Did he say, "Oh God, I'm in trouble. Please help me. Please get me out of this one. Please, please, please"? Did he beg and plead? No, he prayed a simple prayer. "Let it be known this day that thou art God in Israel, and that I am thy servant" (1 Kings 18:36). His prayer lasted less than a minute, and the fire came down from heaven in the sight of all the people.

If you stopped right there, you could agree that "Sherry" was right. One simple request is all it takes to receive whatever God is going to do in your behalf.

But the story of Elijah wasn't over yet! Do you remember what happened after the fire had consumed the sacrifice and the wood and the stones of the altar and the water in the trench around the altar? There was still some unfinished business. The crisis on Mount Carmel was precipitated by the fact that there had been no rain for three and a half years. Spectacular as the fire from heaven was, there was still no rain when it had done its work.

Before the rain came, Elijah had to go alone to the top of the mountain, away from the crowds and the intensity of the day. Taking his servant with him, he prayed for rain, then sent his servant to look for a cloud as a token that God was responding to his prayer.

The little lady who wrote all the books makes this comment:

> When upon Mt. Carmel he [Elijah] offered the prayer for rain, his faith was tested, but he persevered in making known his request unto God. Six times he prayed earnestly, and yet there was no sign that his petition was granted, but with a strong faith he urged his plea to the throne of grace. Had he given up in discouragement at the sixth time, his prayer would not have been answered, but he persevered till the answer came (Ellen G. White Comments, *SDA Bible Commentary,* vol. 2, p. 1034).

Notice that the Bible heroes didn't pray (perhaps even pray several times) and then conclude, because there was no apparent response, that God had said No. Their prayers ended at the point of response from God—which invariably came, even though at times the response was No. Elijah held out for a *definite response*. We'll talk more about this later.

Elijah not only kept praying until his prayer was answered, but we are given the insight that had he failed to persevere, the answer would have been different. That's a solemn thought, isn't it?

Why did he persevere? Was it to change God? Was it to wear God out with his petitions, so that God would finally give in, reluctantly, and grant his request? No. That's not the kind of God we serve.

We will take a longer look at the reasons why persistence is a condition for answered prayer in a separate chapter. For now, simply notice the Bible premise that we are to persevere in bringing our requests before God, and there are Bible examples of the fact that if we settle for asking only once, there may be times when the answer would be different than if we had continued to press our petitions before His throne until He responded.

A spirit of forgiveness

Right in the middle of the Lord's prayer we find the statement, "Forgive us our debts, as we forgive our debtors" (Matthew 6:12). Jesus once told the strange story of a servant who owed a large debt to the king—an overwhelming debt, in fact. He had no money to pay, and so the king ordered him sent off to prison. But the man pleaded for more time, and, overcome with compassion, the king forgave him his entire debt, right up front!

As he was leaving the palace of the king a free man, this servant happened to run into a fellow servant who owed him a small sum. Now maybe the servant wanted to pay the king back. Maybe he thought it would be a good idea to start saving in case such a thing ever happened again, so he wouldn't have to be at the mercy of the king in the future. Whatever the reason, the king's servant demanded the money owed to him. And when his fellow servant couldn't pay immediately, the king's servant had him cast into prison.

Someone happened to see this little drama, and it upset him. He hurried back to the king and told him all that had taken place. The king was upset too—so upset, in fact, that he re-called the forgiven servant and took back his forgiveness! The moral of the story is, "So likewise shall my heavenly Father do also unto you, if ye from your hearts forgive not every one his brother their trespasses" (Matthew 18:35).

Do you like the story? Do you like the "moral" of the story? Are you glad that God is going to treat you as the king treated his unforgiving servant? Is this good news, or bad news?

It was bad news for the first servant, when he found out that he was going to be put in prison for a debt he couldn't pay. It was good news when he heard that the king wasn't going to demand payment.

It was bad news for the second servant, who was sent to prison for a much smaller debt than that of the first servant. The first servant may have thought it was good news to see the second servant thrown in prison, but it was bad news when the king cancelled his pardon and sent him to prison after all. No doubt it was good news for the second servant, sitting alone in the prison cell, when he saw the first servant being brought in to join him! That was bad news for the first servant, but it was good news for the people of the kingdom, when they saw that justice had been done.

So whether you think the story was good news or bad news depends on who you are, and where you are in the story, doesn't it?

This story illustrates what I call the "so long as" principle. So long as you are accepting God's forgiveness for yourself, you *will be* forgiving toward your brother. When you are unforgiving toward others, it is merely an indication that you are no longer accepting the forgiveness God has offered to you. This first servant in the parable may have once accepted the king's forgiveness, though he never expressed appreciation so far as we know, so perhaps he never accepted it in the first place. But we know what he did with the king's pardon at the point in the story where he sent his fellow servant off to the cell. He refused the king's forgiveness at that time, regardless of what he did before.

God is not pushy. He does not force His forgiveness on anyone. If we refuse His forgiveness, and by this means keep an unforgiving spirit ourselves, He accepts our choice in the matter and doesn't crowd us with His blessings.

This parable is talking about more than surface forgiveness, for in the "moral" of the story, it says, "if ye from your *hearts* forgive not." The only way we can have forgiveness for others in our hearts is to accept God's forgiveness, in our hearts, for ourselves.

Go where prayer is made

Where is prayer made? First of all, in your own closet. Secret prayer is the first step toward effective prayer. Those who pray in secret will be openly rewarded. Family prayer or group prayer or public prayer will be only as effective as the effectiveness of the secret prayer life of those who gather together. Prayer always begins one-to-one with God.

However, group prayer is important. The body of Christ is important. *Steps to Christ* says that those who are really seeking for communion with God will be seen in the prayer meeting (p. 98). Those who are really seeking for communion with God will watch for every opportunity to meet together with others and unite with them in prayer.

Each of us is invited to bring our requests to the Lord privately. But there are other invitations for extra power in prayer.

> If two of you shall agree on earth as touching any thing that they shall ask, it shall be done for them of my Father which is in heaven. For where two or three are gathered together in my name, there am I in the midst of them (Matthew 18:19, 20).

There is power in numbers! Even in little numbers—numbers as small as two and three! One reason why group prayers can be more effective may be that it helps God solve one of His biggest problems—human beings taking glory to themselves for the work He has done for and through them. If you and I both pray for the same thing, and God grants our requests, neither of us will be quite so tempted to take the credit to ourselves, for it might have been your prayer that God was able to answer—or it might have been mine. Who can know?

Another factor in public and group prayers is found in the Old Testament. God is pleased when we all go to His house together and offer prayer to Him. You can read about it in 2 Chronicles 6:24-31. The people of Israel were instructed that if they were under attack from an enemy or if there was no rain or if there was a plague in the land, they could come to the house of God and spread out their case before the Lord, and He would hear from heaven, forgive their sin, and answer their petition.

Pray everywhere, about everything, all the time

Unlimited prayer is the most effective! We are invited to be constantly in an attitude of prayer, so that our thoughts will turn toward God spontaneously, at any unexpected trial, or at any time we need His grace. We are invited to be continually aware of His blessings, to maintain an attitude of praise and thanksgiving to Him, and to be always mindful of His mercies. The more of our life we share with God, the more of His response, counsel, and wisdom will be given us in return. Do you want more answers to prayer? The answer is to pray more! God is not like a fairy godmother who offers to fulfill three wishes, and no more! He has unlimited resources, and He invites us to continually reach out to Him for His grace and power in every aspect of our lives.

Unceasing prayer does not mean unceasing conversation. When you are with a friend or family member, you don't have to talk all the time in order to be communicating. You can communicate through silence, through shared activities, through spending time together. The same is true in your friendship with God. You don't have to talk all the time to be involved in unceasing prayer. But He can be your unseen Companion in all of your daily life.

Pray and work

God does not want us to become hermits, withdraw from the world, and devote our full time to prayer. Jesus' life is our example. He lived between the mountain and the multitude. He spent His days with the crowds, healing and teaching and ministering to their needs. But He always found time— several hours each day, in fact—when He could be alone with His Father. In the early morning or in the quiet of the evening, He would go apart from the people who followed Him and seek strength in communion with heaven.

One reason why some people have trouble with their devotional lives is that they are not working. Anytime we try to eat without exercising the result is deadly, in our spiritual life as much as in our physical life. In fact, probably in nine cases out of ten when someone complains of a devotional life that has gone sour, the reason is that he has failed to get involved in outreach and ministry to others. In order to have a healthy prayer life, we must be involved in Christian service. The two always go together.

To pray and work is an important condition for answered prayer. We will look further into this subject in the chapter on "Prayer and Witness."

Ask in the name of Jesus

We cannot come before the Father in our own righteousness. All of the checks that we present to the heavenly bank to be cashed have to be signed by God's Son, Jesus. There is still power in the name of Jesus, and we are invited to bring our requests and petitions in His name.

However, praying in the name of Jesus is more than "a mere mention of that name at the beginning and the ending of a prayer. It is to pray in the mind and spirit of Jesus, while we believe His promises, rely upon His grace, and work His works" (*Steps to Christ*, pp. 100, 101).

Because of the deeper meaning of asking in Jesus' name, it is impossible to pray in His name in our own strength. The only way we can pray in the mind and spirit of Jesus, the only way we can trust in His promises and work His works, is for Him to live His life in us. To pray in the name of Jesus, we must be in close relationship with Him.

God's invitation to bring our requests before Him in the name of Jesus does not mean that He is unwilling to hear and bless us. Jesus said:

> At that day ye shall ask in my name: and I say not unto you, that I will pray the Father for you: for the Father himself loveth you, because ye have loved me, and have believed that I came out from God (John 16:26, 27).

Jesus spoke of the willingness of earthly parents to give good gifts to their children, and then asked, "How much more shall your heavenly Father give the Holy Spirit to them that ask him?" (Luke 11:13).

So the entire Godhead is involved. We are to pray to the Father, in the name of the Son, and ask for the gift of the Holy Spirit—who inspires our prayers and presents them before the Father in our behalf. All heaven is interested in responding to our prayers!

Thanksgiving and praise

The psalms are filled with praises to God. You can find many examples. We will notice two here: "Oh that men would praise the Lord for his goodness, and for his wonderful works to the children of men!" "I will praise thee, O Lord, among the people: and I will sing praises unto thee among the nations" (Psalms 107:8; 108:3).

> Our devotional exercises should not consist wholly in asking and receiving. Let us not be always thinking of our wants and never of the benefits we receive. We do not pray any too much, but we are too sparing of giving thanks. We are the constant recipients of God's mercies, and yet how little gratitude we express, how little we praise Him for what He has done for us (*Steps to Christ*, pp. 102, 103).

Why is praise and thanksgiving so important? Because through praise and thanksgiving we place the glory of God where it belongs and keep from taking His glory to ourselves. Also, it is very difficult to praise and thank God for His blessings and at the same time feel sad, gloomy, and discontented! God wants us to find joy in service for Him. He wants us to rejoice in our relationship with Him. After all, He rejoices in His relationship with us! He says, "Behold my servant, whom I uphold; mine elect, in whom my soul delighteth." "The Lord thy God in the midst of thee is mighty; he will save, he will rejoice over thee with joy; he will rest in his love, he will joy over thee with singing" (Isaiah 42:1; Zephaniah 3:17).

Did you know that God delights in you? Did you know that

He rejoices over you so much that He will burst into song because of His joy in you? Think about that: The God of the universe singing about you because He is so happy about you! And He invites you to find joy and delight in *Him*. "Delight thyself also in the Lord; and he shall give thee the desires of thine heart" (Psalm 37:4).

Chapter 7

Prayer and Cherished Sin

Behold, the Lord's hand is not shortened, that it cannot save; neither his ear heavy, that it cannot hear: but your iniquities have separated between you and your God, and your sins have hid his face from you, that he will not hear (Isaiah 59:1, 2).

If I regard iniquity in my heart, the Lord will not hear me (Psalm 66:18).

These are two of the devil's favorite Bible texts, and he quotes them every chance he gets! Do you doubt that the devil quotes Bible texts? Look at his temptations presented to Jesus, when Jesus was in the wilderness. The devil quoted Scripture. Quoting Scripture to candy-coat his temptations is one of the devil's long-standing practices, and I would like to suggest that these two texts are among his favorites.

This is not to say that the Holy Spirit does not also make use of these texts to convict of sin. But the Holy Spirit's conviction will always encourage us to come *to* God as the only remedy for our sinful condition. If you ever started to pray, then suddenly remembered these two texts and stopped right there because you were afraid you were too much of a sinner to come to God, then you have heard the devil quoting these scriptures in your ear.

But before we go any further, let's make a list of a few things we are *not* trying to say in this chapter. That way we will avoid any misunderstandings as we get into our subject.

1. We are *not* saying that it is OK to sin.
2. We are *not* saying that God overlooks or excuses sin.
3. We are *not* saying that victory is impossible or unnecessary.
4. We are *not* saying that it doesn't make any difference to answered prayer whether or not you are involved in sin.
5. We are *not* saying that you have to be just about ready for translation before you can pray effectively.
6. We are *not* saying that it is your righteousness or your obedience or your victory that enables God to answer your prayers.

We need to have a clear definition of sin before we discuss the effect of sin on answers to prayer. We must not define sin in terms of behavior only. Rather, we should always define sin in terms of relationship. Sin means living life apart from God. Sin is separation from God. This results in sins—breaking the commandments, outward unrighteousness, wrong behavior. But the root of the sin problem is always a broken relationship. Sinful behavior is only the result. Jesus said:

> This is the condemnation, that light is come into the world, and men loved darkness rather than light, because their deeds were evil. For every one that doeth evil hateth the light, neither cometh to the light, lest his deeds should be reproved (John 3:19, 20).

If you would like a definition for "cherished sin," try this one: *Cherished sin is any sin that causes you to scrap your relationship with Christ in order to carry on the sin.* Here's another definition: *Cherished sin is when you deliberately stay away from the Light because you don't want your deeds to be reproved.* It is *not* cherished sin when you fall and fail and sin because of weakness and immaturity. It is not cherished sin so long as you keep coming to the Light, because you want more than anything else to allow Him to lead you to victory over your sins and failings. "Errors committed through ignorance, thoughtlessness, or weakness are not willful, premeditated sin" (*Testimonies*, vol. 5, p. 605).

When David was fleeing from Saul, he became so weary of the struggle that he lost his hold upon God. He sinned by going to the Philistines, who were the enemies of God's people, and entering into a covenant with them for his own protection. God was dishonored by David's unbelief.

Before long, David was placed in a difficult position because of his course of action. The Philistines decided to go to war against Israel and told David that they expected him to join them in their battle. But notice this comment about David's predicament:

> David was caused to feel that he had missed his path. Far better would it have been for him to find refuge in God's strong fortresses of the mountains than with the avowed enemies of Jehovah and His people. But the Lord in His great mercy did not punish this error of His servant by leaving him to himself in his distress and perplexity; for though David, losing his grasp on divine power, had faltered and turned aside from the path of strict integrity, it was still the purpose of his heart to be true to God (*Patriarchs and Prophets*, p. 690).

David had sinned—but he was not guilty of *cherished* sin. His heart was still inclined toward God. He did not refuse to come to the Light. To the contrary, because he kept coming to the Light, he was shown the error of his way and led to repentance.

We can be absolutely certain of one thing: Whatever the Bible means by prayers that cannot be answered because we regard iniquity in our hearts; whatever it means by sins that separate us from God so that He cannot hear our prayers, it can never mean prayers of repentance and confession. If we were unable to turn to God and seek His grace to deal with the iniquity in our hearts, we would be without hope. Of ourselves, there is no way we can ever remove the iniquity from our own hearts. Only God's power can accomplish that for us. And God is very patient with us as we grow, as we try to learn how to surrender the control of our lives to Him.

The disciples bickered and argued the entire three and a half years they walked with Jesus. They knew what they were doing. They knew it was wrong. They lingered along the wayside so that Jesus would get far enough ahead of them that He could not hear what they were saying! Have you ever, in your relationship with God, tried to keep enough distance between you and Him so that He wouldn't realize what you were thinking or doing? It doesn't work, does it? It didn't work for the disciples, either. Jesus knew, in spite of their precautions. He rebuked them, He counseled with them—and He continued walking with them. The disciples sinned, but they did not cherish their sins, in spite of the fact that for a time they seemed to fall into the same sin over and over again. They were not cherishing sin, because they kept coming to the Light and seeking the Light, instead of running from it. In the end, instead of scrapping their relationship with Christ in favor of sin, every disciple except Judas scrapped his sins in favor of the relationship. Only Judas was guilty of cherished sin; he went out and hanged himself. Because he was unwilling to surrender himself to the God above, he surrendered himself to the dogs beneath.

During the three and a half years that the disciples worked side by side with Jesus they prayed for the sick, cast out demons, and were even given power to raise the dead! Jesus told them that their names were written in heaven. Yet they didn't experience victory, all of the time, even over "known" sin.

Instead, their victory, like their dependence upon Christ, was on-again, off-again. One moment they would depend upon Christ and experience His power in their lives. The next moment they would depend upon themselves and sin again. One minute Jesus could commend Peter for saying, "Thou art the Christ, the Son of the living God." The next minute He would say, "Get thee behind me, Satan" (Matthew 16:16, 23). One minute Peter could walk on water. The next instant he was sinking beneath the angry waves. The moment after that, he was walking on water again!

It took a period of time, in their experience of coming to the Light, for the disciples to learn faith and dependence. But they kept coming to the Light, and in the end the result of the Light at work in their lives was manifest.

But the point that particularly interests us here is that the disciples did not have to wait until they had reached Christian maturity to have their prayers answered. Even their prayers for things other than repentance and forgiveness were answered from the beginning of their walk with Jesus. They did not have to wait until His death and resurrection had passed. They did not have to wait until after the outpouring of the Spirit at Pentecost.

On the other hand, did it make a difference when their faith and trust in God finally matured and they received the baptism of the Spirit? Of course it did!

Had the disciples decided to wait until they could know the ultimate experience of prayer before beginning to pray, they would never have known the power of prayer at all. They had to start at the beginning and allow time for the fruits of the Spirit to develop in their lives. And we today must do the same thing.

We are not to be so overwhelmed with the thought of our sins and errors that we shall cease to pray. Some realize their great weakness and sin, and become discouraged. Satan casts his dark shadow between them and the Lord Jesus, their atoning sacrifice. They say, It is useless for me to pray. My prayers are so mingled with evil thoughts that the Lord will not hear them. . . . Many, not understanding that their doubts come from Satan, become faint-hearted, and are defeated in the conflict. Do not, because your thoughts are evil, cease to pray. If we could in our own wisdom and strength pray aright, we could also live aright, and would need no atoning sacrifice (Ellen G. White, *Signs of the Times*, November 18, 1903).

Without the privilege of prayer, we have no hope of ever reaching the place where we can pray effectively! It is through the avenue of prayer that victory over sin is received. It is through prayer that we are brought into fellowship with heaven. It is through prayer that our hearts are changed. We have been told that when it is hardest to pray, that is when we should pray the hardest. The less worthy we feel, the less right we have to come to the throne of grace, the more desperately we need to pray.

The devil works hard to prevent us from praying because he knows that prayer is the secret of power in the Christian life.

> The adversary seeks continually to obstruct the way to the mercy seat, that we may not by earnest supplication and faith obtain grace and power to resist temptation (*Steps to Christ*, p. 95).

The devil comes to you with a temptation to sin, and he says, "Sin is no big deal. God isn't that particular. Haven't you heard? It's easier to get forgiveness than permission. Go ahead and do your own thing. You can always say you're sorry afterward."

Then, as soon as you yield, he shakes his head and says, "*Now* you've done it. You really blew it this time. God will never forgive something *this* terrible. There's no point in even asking for forgiveness—no point in even trying to pray. Haven't you heard? God can't hear your prayers when you have iniquity in your heart."

And too often, we end up listening to him—both times! We don't notice that he's changed his story, as all liars do—and we're afraid to pray, afraid to seek God's help, because we know we have sinned.

Reaping what you sow

A group of us were having a Sabbath afternoon discussion one time, and someone said, "If you do something you know is wrong and you get yourself into trouble, then you can't expect

God to come and deliver you from *that*. He may be willing to accept you back again, as far as eternal life is concerned, when you repent. But you have to reap the results of what you have done."

Do you believe that? Do you believe in the law of the harvest, that whatever you sow, that's what you are going to reap? You may find comfort in the fact that God is willing to walk with you while you reap. But is God ever going to answer your prayers for a crop of good oats after you have sown your wild oats? Aren't we told that if we sow to the wind, we reap the whirlwind?

Psalm 107 presents four scenarios. It describes four types of people. First are those who have been exiled. They are wandering in the wilderness, hungry and thirsty, and they have no city to dwell in. The second group are rebels, sitting in darkness, bound in affliction and iron. Their hearts have been brought down with labor. They have fallen and there is no one to help them. The third group are fools. Their affliction is the result of their own foolishness, their own iniquities. The fourth group are ordinary people going about their everyday tasks. They are sailors and fishermen who went down to the sea in ships to do business, but they ran into heavy storms and are at their wits' end.

These four groups—the exiled, the rebels, the fools, and the workers—have one thing in common that is repeated at the end of each scenario. You can find it in verses 6, 13, 19, and 28. It makes no difference whether their troubles are the result of their own foolishness, of their own rebellion, or simply a result of living in a world of sin. One answer fits all:

Then they cried unto the Lord in their trouble, and he saved them out of their distresses.

On a practical level, it may not make a lot of difference whether your foolishness caused the problems and the crises that you face today, because no matter who's to blame, the solution is the same: Go to the Lord with your trouble. He has power to save—even fools and rebels.

Rules Versus Laws

In his book *Sit, Walk, Stand,* Watchman Nee distinguishes between a rule and a law. An example of a rule would be the 55 m.p.h. speed limit. We refer to it as a law, but it's not, really, because it is possible to go faster then 55 m.p.h. You have probably done it many times without getting caught, getting into an accident, or having your car disintegrate on the highway. The fact that the government asks us to drive 55 m.p.h. does not mean that it is impossible to drive faster. Speed limits are rules, not laws.

In contrast, consider gravity. The law of gravity works on Sunday and on Thursday and on Monday afternoon. It doesn't matter whether anyone is watching. It works equally for the common man, for kings, and for presidents. No one is exempt. The law of gravity is inflexible. There is no getting around the law of gravity. It is more than a recommendation or counsel or good advice. It is more than a rule. It is a law. Do you see the difference?

There is only one way to get around a law. You can't ignore it, but you may find a greater law that outweighs it. Is there a law greater than the law of gravity? Yes, there is a law which says that anything lighter than air goes up. That's the law that keeps helium balloons in the air at a picnic! The law about something lighter than air going up is greater than the law of gravity. It is as natural for a helium balloon to go up as it is natural for an apple to fall down.

The same principle applies to spiritual laws. Paul talks about two spiritual laws in Romans 7 and 8. Look first at Romans 7, where he has just finished expressing his frustration over the discovery that the good he wants to do he doesn't do, while the evil that he doesn't want to do is the very thing he ends up doing. Verse 21 says, "I find then a *law*, that, when I would do good, evil is present with me." Paul was grappling with the law of sin and death, which, like the law of gravity, was forcing him downward. All of us who are born into this world of sin are subject to that law. Even when we want to do good, evil is present with us. *It's a law.*

But here's the good news! There is a law that is greater than the law of Romans 7:21. It's found in Romans 8:2: "The *law* of the Spirit of life in Christ Jesus hath made me free from the law of sin and death" (emphasis supplied). Even though the law of sin and death is as certain as the law of gravity, there is another, greater law—the law of the spirit of life in Christ Jesus—which can set us free from the effects of the first law.

With this in mind, let's go back to the first two texts of this chapter, Isaiah 59 and Psalm 66. When we are told, "If I regard iniquity in my heart, the Lord will not hear me," are we talking about a rule or a law? Which do you think?

Do you remember the blind man of John 9—the one who had been blind from birth? After he had been healed, he was called before the Jewish leaders to explain what happened. He said, "Now we know that God heareth not sinners: but if any man be a worshipper of God, and doeth his will, him he heareth" (verse 31). Was he speaking the truth or not?

It is a law that God does not hear sinners, that He does not answer those who have iniquity in their hearts. But there is good news. There is a greater law—in fact, there are several greater laws that we can consider in this connection.

The first greater law says that God's mercy exceeds His justice. If God were looking for an excuse to do away with this sinful world, He could have done it long ago. But His mercy is extended to every one who turns to Him for help—and there is no waiting period! We don't have to put in a certain amount of time doing good behavior to get Him to help us. As soon as we come to Him, He accepts us. Jesus said, "Whoever comes to me I will never drive away" (John 6:37, NIV).

Some seem to feel that they must be on probation, and must prove to the Lord that they are reformed, before they can claim His blessing. But they may claim the blessing of God even now. They must have His grace, the Spirit of Christ, to help their infirmities, or they cannot resist evil. Jesus loves to have us come to Him just as we are, sinful, helpless, dependent. We may come with all our weakness, our folly, our sinfulness, and fall at His feet in penitence. It is His glory to encircle us in the arms of His love and to bind up our wounds, to cleanse us from all impurity (*Steps to Christ*, p. 52).

The law of the mercy of God, extended with *no waiting period*, is one of the greater laws that supersedes the one about regarding iniquity in the heart. This greater law of God's mercy explains why the disciples could heal the sick, cast out devils, and raise the dead, and still not be perfect. The reason is that anytime they turned to Christ, they were accepted immediately. They did not have to stay surrendered to Him for so many weeks or days or hours or even minutes before presenting their requests for blessings. He went to work on their behalf immediately.

Remember their experience at the foot of the Mount of Transfiguration? The disciples were depending on themselves instead of Jesus. They were ashamed and surprised to discover that their prayer for the healing of the demon-possessed boy was not answered. Not only did they lack faith, but so did the boy's father, who initiated the request.

Then Jesus came, and they cried to Him for help. They realized their need. The boy's father said, "I thought I believed, but evidently I don't believe enough. Please help me with my unbelief." And the boy was healed (see Matthew 17:14-21).

A second law that is greater than the law about regarding iniquity in the heart is the law of God's glory. This is the law that Moses pleaded in Exodus 32:12. The people of Israel were disqualified for God's help because of the law of sin and death, but Moses pleaded a greater law as the reason why God should not destroy Israel:

Wherefore should the Egyptians speak, and say, For mischief did he bring them out, to slay them in the mountains, and to consume them from the face of the earth? Turn from thy fierce wrath, and repent of this evil against thy people.

Many times in the history of our world this second, greater law, has been in operation, and the judgments that God could have sent to fulfill the first law were averted because of the second law, His name and glory and reputation on the earth.

A third law that is greater than the law about regarding iniquity in the heart is the law that God is able to respond when He is called upon to intervene. We're back again to the fact that *it is always right to ask.* Abraham went down to Egypt, where he lied about Sarah's being his wife, and he got into trouble. But he called upon God to deliver him, and God was able to respond because one of His children had appealed to Him. Abraham was in the wrong—yet he was delivered. You can read about it in Genesis 12:11-20—and *again* in Genesis 20! For, you see, Abraham didn't learn his lesson the first time. He did the same thing again, and again God delivered him, in spite of the fact that he brought on the problem by his own sin.

Samson is another example of this third, greater law. Samson was a rascal! Have you read his story lately? Study Judges 13 through 16. Samson sinned repeatedly, but when he turned and called upon the name of the Lord, God delivered him.

What about Esther? Have you looked at her life lately? We tend to think of Esther as a rival to Mary, Jesus' mother, for purity and integrity. But she married an idolatrous king, which God's people had been specifically warned not to do, and she had sexual relations with him even before she married him! Also, she concealed the fact that she was one of God's people. But when she prayed for God's people, God heard her prayer and used her to deliver them.

Look at Balaam. He was not only a professed follower of God, but was a prophet as well. Look at the history of Israel. Look at Simon the Pharisee, who was healed from his leprosy *before* he was converted and *before* he accepted Jesus as his Saviour.

Sometimes we make it seem far too difficult to approach God. We think that we have to be all but ready for translation before we can bring our requests before Him and expect a response. Perhaps we do this to emphasize the importance of victory and obedience and overcoming. But I think you will agree that it is safe to stay with the Bible on this subject.

Read 2 Chronicles 6:24-31. God was giving special instruction to the people of Israel, and He went out of His way to let them know that even when they had sinned, they were still invited into His presence. They were invited to ask for His deliverance from the *punishment* and *results* of their transgression—not just for forgiveness and eternal life. It's a rather long passage, but it's worth the time to consider it. We'll begin with verse 24:

> If thy people Israel be put to the worse before the enemy, *because they have sinned against thee*; and shall return and confess thy name, and pray and make supplication before thee in this house; then hear thou from the heavens, and forgive the sin of thy people Israel, and bring them again unto the land which thou gavest to them and to their fathers.

> When the heaven is shut up, and there is no rain, *because they have sinned against thee*; yet if they pray toward this place, and confess thy name, and turn from their sin, when thou dost afflict them; then hear thou from heaven, and forgive the sin of thy servants, and of thy people Israel, when thou hast taught them the good way, wherein they should walk; and send rain upon thy land, which thou hast given unto thy people for an inheritance (emphasis supplied).

The promises continue on to the end of the chapter, even offering the same blessing to the stranger who has heard about the great name of God and who comes and prays, seeking His blessing. Skip down to verse 36:

> *If they sin against thee*, (for there is no man which sinneth not,) and thou be angry with them, and deliver them over before their enemies, and they carry them away captives unto a land far off or near; yet if they bethink themselves in the land whither they are carried

captive, and turn and pray unto thee in the land of their captivity, saying, We have sinned, we have done amiss, and have dealt wickedly; if they return to thee with all their heart and with all their soul in the land of their captivity, whither they have carried them captives, and pray toward their land, which thou gavest unto their fathers, . . . then hear thou from the heavens, even from thy dwelling place, their prayer and their supplications, and maintain their cause, and forgive thy people which have sinned against thee (2 Chronicles 6:36-39, emphasis supplied).

God has done everything a God of love knows how to do in order to make it as easy as possible for us, hasn't He? He has worked time and again to deliver, and help, and heal when people had no right to His blessing. In fact, none of us are given what we deserve, or we wouldn't be alive right now. Not one of us deserves heaven or eternal life or the least of God's mercies.

Do you worry that applying God's greater laws will lead to license? You needn't be concerned. If God is willing to take that chance, why should we hesitate? We have been told that God's lovingkindness and mercy leads us to repentance. When we understand His mercy and love in our own experience, our hearts will be broken, and we will be drawn to Him.

Chapter 8
Prayer and Overcoming

When my son was in college, he was interested in rock climbing. One time he went rock climbing in Yosemite with a friend of his, an older man, and on the climb up a cliff they dropped their canteen.

The day was hot, and the climb was a long one. In fact, they spent the night hanging from the ropes. The next day, when they finally reached the top, both of them were dehydrated. In fact, they were so desperately in need of water that they could hardly walk. The older man gasped, "Get me water. Money is no object!" And he lay there, unable to move farther.

My son left him and managed to struggle to the edge of a creek some distance away. Later he described how wonderful that drink of water tasted. It made me thirsty just to hear about it!

He found renewed energy after he drank and was able to take some water back to his friend. Both of them recovered— although my son was so dehydrated that he lost over twenty pounds!

Water is a wonderful gift. For most of us, most of the time, it is so readily and abundantly available that we fail to appreciate what it would be like not to have all of it that we need.

The Bible talks a lot about water. Water is often used as a symbol of spiritual life. Isaiah said:

> Ho, every one that thirsteth, come ye to the waters, and he that hath no money; come ye, buy, and eat; yea,

come, buy wine and milk without money and without price (Isaiah 55:1).

Notice the words of Jesus: "Blessed are they which do hunger and *thirst* after righteousness"; "he that believeth on me shall never *thirst*" (Matthew 5:6; John 6:35, emphasis supplied). He said to the woman at the well:

Whosoever drinketh of the water that I shall give him shall never thirst; but the water that I shall give him shall be in him a well of water springing up into everlasting life (John 4:14).

To the multitude in the temple Jesus said, "If any man thirst, let him come unto me, and drink" (John 7:37). And in Revelation 22:17 He again makes the offer, "Let him that is athirst come. And whosoever will, let him take the water of life freely." Heaven is described as a place with plenty of water:

They shall hunger no more, neither thirst any more; neither shall the sun light on them, nor any heat. For the Lamb which is in the midst of the throne shall feed them, and shall lead them unto living fountains of water: and God shall wipe away all tears from their eyes (Revelation 7:16, 17).

God used water to teach the people of Israel important lessons about their need for him and their dependence upon Him for salvation:

[Thou] gavest them bread from heaven for their hunger, and broughtest forth water for them out of the rock for their thirst, and promisedst them that they should go in to possess the land which thou hadst sworn to give them (Nehemiah 9:15).

They thirsted not when he led them through the

deserts: he caused the waters to flow out of the rock for them: he clave the rock also, and the waters gushed out (Isaiah 48:21).

Let's go back to the time of Israel's wanderings in the wilderness, and consider the two times that water was brought forth out of the rock for them. In the process, we can discover surprising help on the subject of prayer and overcoming.

Water from the rock, part 1

God first brought water from the rock shortly after the Israelites left the land of Egypt. They had already seen the parting of the Red Sea, the waters of Marah changed from bitter to sweet, and the manna sent to supply their need for food. Now, when they reached Rephidim, there was no water. The supplies they had brought with them were running low, so the people did their usual thing. They began to complain. They lamented the fact that they had left Egypt, and they blamed Moses for the problem. In fact, they were so upset with him that they were ready to stone him.

So Moses did *his* usual thing: He fell on his knees. Let's read the story:

> Moses cried unto the Lord, saying, What shall I do unto this people? they be almost ready to stone me. And the Lord said unto Moses, Go on before the people, and take with thee of the elders of Israel; and thy rod, wherewith thou smotest the river, take in thine hand, and go. Behold, I will stand before thee there upon the rock in Horeb; and thou shalt smite the rock, and there shall come water out of it, that thy people may drink. And Moses did so in the sight of the elders of Israel. And he called the name of the place Massah, and Meribah, because of the chiding of the children of Israel, and because they tempted the Lord, saying Is the Lord among us, or not? (Exodus 17:4-7).

This miraculous provision for the people's needs was intended to give them more than just water! God was teaching them lessons they needed to learn and helping them to unlearn many of the misconceptions they had acquired during their stay in Egypt.

It was a sandbox illustration, if you please, of the great truth of justification by faith. The Rock was a symbol of Christ. Paul said, "[They] did all drink the same spiritual drink: for they drank of that spiritual Rock that followed them: and that Rock was Christ" (1 Corinthians 10:4).

The striking of the Rock represented the death of Christ for sin. "Christ was once offered to bear the sins of many" (Hebrews 9:28). When Christ died on the cross, once for all, salvation became available for all. Justification means salvation for the weakest, the most sinful, the most undeserving, the most helpless. We do not receive it because of our own merit, or our own righteousness, but through Jesus Christ, our Saviour and Advocate. Because of the cross, we can come to the Rock, Christ Jesus, and be presented before the Father, forgiven and accepted. In fact, *more* than forgiveness is offered. Because of the cross, we can accept the sacrifice of Jesus in our behalf and stand before the Father as though we had never sinned. That's justification, and it's beautiful!

But there was more to come! Salvation includes more than justification. It also includes sanctification—and ultimately glorification when Jesus comes again. Even after the Israelites had accepted the water of life and the forgiveness provided—even after they had chosen to become God's people—there was still more to learn about salvation.

The author of Hebrews talks about it in chapter 4 when he describes the further "rest" for the people of God. Not only are we to rest from our own attempts to save ourselves from the *guilt* of sin; we are also to rest from our attempts to save ourselves from the *power* of sin. Not only are we incapable of bringing about our own forgiveness; we are incapable of bringing about our own obedience! Paul said, "There remaineth therefore a rest to the people of God. For he that is entered into his rest, he also hath ceased from his own works, as God did from his" (Hebrews 4:9, 10).

The people of Israel were slow to enter into this rest. It seemed hard for them to understand, and even harder for them to experience. Even Moses had trouble knowing the experience all the time, as we see from the story in Numbers 20, when water was brought from the rock for the second time.

Water from the rock, part 2

Thirty-eight years later, near the end of their wandering in the wilderness, God brought forth water from the rock again. You can read the story in Numbers 20. The Bible says:

> Then came the children of Israel, even the whole congregation, into the desert of Zin in the first month: and the people abode in Kadesh; and Miriam died there, and was buried there. And there was no water for the congregation: and they gathered themselves together against Moses and against Aaron (verses 1, 2).

These people hadn't changed much in thirty-eight years, had they? They were still the same "generation of gripers," still blaming Moses for all their troubles. It should have been good news that the supply of water was about exhausted. There was water in abundance in the Promised Land, and the end of the miraculous water supply in the desert was an indication that they were going straight into Canaan. But the people missed the signpost and began to complain about the good news! "And the people chode with Moses, and spake, saying, Would God that we had died when our brethren died before the Lord!" (verse 3).

Who were they referring to here? Apparently there were still some left alive, twenty years old and upward, who remembered when Korah, Dathan, and Abiram died as a result of the judgments of God on their rebellion and conspiracy. They said:

> Why have ye brought up the congregation of the Lord into this wilderness, that we and our cattle should die there? And wherefore have ye made us to come up out of

Egypt, to bring us in unto this evil place? it is no place of seed, or of figs, or of vines, or of pomegranates; neither is there any water to drink. And Moses and Aaron went from the presence of the assembly unto the door of the tabernacle of the congregation, and they fell upon their faces: and the glory of the Lord appeared unto them. And the Lord spake unto Moses, saying, Take the rod . . . (Numbers 20:4-8).

Why do you suppose God said that? He should have told Moses to leave the rod at home! Moses would have been better off without the rod that day—or would he? Does God take away every opportunity for temptation? No, for if He did, He would be tampering with our power of choice, and that is one thing God will never do. So God told Moses to:

Take the rod, and gather thou the assembly together, thou, and Aaron thy brother, and speak ye unto the rock before their eyes; and it shall give forth his water, and thou shalt bring forth to them water out of the rock: so thou shalt give the congregation and their beasts drink. And Moses took the rod from before the Lord, as he commanded him. And Moses and Aaron gathered the congregation together before the rock, and he said unto them, Hear now, ye rebels; must we fetch you water out of this rock? (verses 8-10).

Was Moses speaking the truth when he called the people rebels? Were they rebels? Yes, they were. Moses had told them before, and he would tell them again, of their rebellious natures. His last words before he left them on the borders of the Promised Land reminded them of it again. He said, "Ye have been rebellious against the Lord from the day that I knew you" (Deuteronomy 9:24). But here at the rock, even though there was truth in his words, Moses spoke in the wrong *spirit*. Have you ever had that happen to you? Have you ever spoken the truth in the wrong spirit? I have been guilty of that many times in dealing with my children. It's easy to feel so pious when the words are right—and to forget that the spirit must also be right in order for the words to carry weight.

Then came the tragic phrase: "Must *we* fetch you water out of this rock?" Must *we*?

Moses had spent the first forty years of his life in Egypt, learning how to kill Egyptians and bury them in the sand. And he got one! Then he had to spend the second forty years of his life herding sheep on the backside of the desert, unlearning what he had learned during the first forty years. Now he is at the end of the third forty years, which he spent wandering with two million illiterate, garlic-smelling slaves, who have consistently blamed him for all their troubles and problems, and who often wanted to crush his skull on the desert rocks. Now, on the borders of the Promised Land—the land flowing with milk and honey, the land toward which Moses' heart has been drawn for almost 120 years—it appears that they are going to blow it again and will have to be sent back for another forty years. No wonder Moses lost his patience. No wonder his faith failed him for the moment, as he considered the stubbornness and rebellion of the people he had been leading.

So he said, "Must *we* fetch you water out of this rock?"

Who were the "we" that he spoke about? Probably the worst interpretation would be to assume that he was speaking of Aaron and himself. "Must Aaron and I bring you water out of the rock?" Of course, with their human power that would have been impossible, and Moses probably knew that, even in this moment of frustration. It is more likely, however, that he was involved in a more subtle error. His "we" probably referred to God and himself. He was talking about bringing water from the rock himself—with God's help. Is that any better? Is it better to say to God, "You do part, and I'll do part"? We're talking about salvation here—not just water on the desert sand.

Sometimes we use the word *cooperation*. But when it comes to the water of life, the water of salvation, God does it *all*. The water from the Rock was *all* God's doing. Moses could not do any part of the work himself.

So this sensitive issue of divine power and human effort

shows up here at the rock in the desert. And it is possible for us today, in our attempts to overcome sin, to strike the rock with Moses. How do we do it? Either by thinking that we have the power in ourselves to live the Christian life—or by thinking that we are to produce obedience with His *help*. Either way is wrong. From beginning to end, salvation, overcoming, victory, and grace are all God's work.

Let's look at a couple of short statements: "All that man can possibly do toward his own salvation is to accept the invitation, 'Whosoever will, let him take the water of life freely' " (*Selected Messages*, bk. 1, p. 343). Add to that the explanation of what these intangible phrases mean: "In communion with Christ, through prayer and the study of the great and precious truths of His word, we shall as hungry souls be fed; as those that thirst, we shall be refreshed at the fountain of life (*Mount of Blessing*, p. 113).

So how do we take the water of life freely? Through communion with Christ in prayer and the study of His Word. That's all we can do toward our own salvation, from beginning to end, including justification, sanctification, and glorification—the whole package. Moses was supposed to speak to the Rock. That was his part. When he did something more than speak to the Rock, he had gone too far. In striking the rock he showed that his trust and dependence on God had failed and that he had taken into his hands that which only God could accomplish.

Speak to the Rock!

What, then, can we do toward our own salvation? We can speak to the Rock! Who is the Rock? As we have already noticed, the Rock is Christ. How do we speak to the Rock? Through prayer. There it is! That is our part. That's what we are to do in order to overcome. We are never to add our own efforts and join Moses in striking the Rock. It's a slap in the face of Jesus to do more than speaking to the Rock. Speaking to the Rock is enough. Anything more is too much.

In part 1 of "Water from the rock" we saw the truth of justification. In part 2 we were given an illustration of sanctification as well. For freedom from the guilt of sin, we come to Christ and ask for His forgiveness. For obedience, victory, and overcoming, we ask for His power. We *speak* to the Rock. Through our relationship with Him, we accept His gifts.

Not only is it a gross misunderstanding to think that the Christian must first be victorious in order to pray; but prayer is in itself the means God has provided to bring forgiveness and power into the Christian's life. Prayer brings victory— even when you are not praying for victory!

It is not necessary to spend your prayer time making a list and checking it twice, focusing on your faults, failures, and sins. In fact, if we spend too much time looking at ourselves, even in prayer, we may become more like ourselves! We may state our needs to Him simply and then go on in fellowship with Him. It is the communion with Him, the association with Him, that changes our lives.

It has been said that a man is known by the company he keeps. We are all influenced by those with whom we associate. The more time we spend with someone, and the more highly we esteem that person, the more his influence is reflected in our lives. The same thing is true in the spiritual life.

Prayer is primarily for communication, as we have already noticed. If prayer were primarily to receive answers from God, in terms of blessings and benefits, then God could have designed prayer to work like the Sears catalog. He would have us supplied with order blanks and a "wish book" to look through to see what was available that would match our needs and desires. We could have filled out the form and stuck it in the mail—or perhaps put it in the offering plate at church! Then we could have sat back and allowed a week to ten days for delivery!

But prayer is for communication. The more you pray, the more time you spend in God's presence. The more time you spend in His presence, the more you are influenced by your communion with Him. By beholding Him, by communicating with Him, you will be changed into His image, into His likeness.

The reverse is also true. When you neglect the privilege of

prayer, when you spend little or no time in communion with Christ, you are drawn away from Him.

The darkness of the evil one encloses those who neglect to pray. The whispered temptations of the enemy entice them to sin; and it is all because they do not make use of the privileges that God has given them in the divine appointment of prayer (*Steps to Christ,* p. 94).

Victory, obedience, and overcoming are His gifts. They are not something we work on, or work up to. They are something we receive, not something we achieve. Do you desire the gift? The only way to obtain the gift is to come into the presence of the Giver. That is the one thing *we* can do. As we do our part, by entering into relationship with Him, by speaking to the Rock, He will do His part, pouring out every needed blessing, exceedingly abundantly above all that we can ask or think.

Chapter 9
Prayer, Faith, and Promises

A few years ago a college student was flying in a small plane with one of the faculty members on school business. When they approached the airport where they were scheduled to land, there was such a dense fog that landing was impossible.

The student had been hearing about faith and claiming Bible promises, and he said, "Watch this! I am going to claim a Bible promise and make this fog go away!"

He whipped out his pocket Bible and turned to one of the verses that appear to give a carte blanche: "Whatsoever ye shall ask in prayer, believing, ye shall receive" (Matthew 21:22).

He claimed the promise, praying that the fog be taken away. The fog did *not* go away, and he was one discouraged student.

Many people have misunderstood the subject of faith, prayer, and Bible promises. We have heard stories like the one about the little girl with the umbrella. Surely everybody has heard that one by now! The town needed rain, and it was announced that there would be a special prayer meeting at the church to pray for rain. On the day of the prayer meeting, when the people gathered together, one little girl brought her umbrella. Everybody smiled at the faith of a little child. But it rained! And the little girl was the only one who didn't get wet on the way home. The obvious conclusion is that God sent the rain because the little girl brought her umbrella.

It is possible to hear these kinds of stories and decide that the way to exercise faith is to get ourselves out on a limb, and then saw off the limb. That will force God to rescue us. The devil delights in this sort of misunderstanding, because it gives him a wonderful opportunity to move in with doubts and questions about God when things don't turn out the way we expect.

Faith is more than positive thinking. Positive thinking will not produce faith. Faith is trust in God, and the only way to develop faith is to learn to know God. Since He is trustworthy, as we learn to know Him, we spontaneously learn to trust Him. Faith is trusting God when things don't turn out the way we expect.

Jesus said that the Father is more willing to give us good gifts than parents are willing to give good things to their children (see Luke 11). Does that picture of God match the idea of a God who would withhold rain until someone showed up with an umbrella? Would a loving God arbitrarily wait for His children to beg and plead and believe hard enough before working in their behalf? Such concepts of faith really show that we think *we* are in charge and that God is under *our* control. We end up trusting more in ourselves and in our attempts to work up the right kind of belief, when we should be trusting in a Father of love who is willing and anxious to give us every needed blessing.

A study of the subject of prayer must necessarily include a study of the nature of true faith. Have you ever prayed—and failed to receive what you desired? What is the explanation that is often given? A lack of faith! Thus you have had to bear not only the disappointment of not receiving what you hoped for, but you take on the added burden of questioning the genuineness of your faith.

It is true that the Bible sometimes mentions faith as an essential ingredient for prayer and receiving God's promises. We could list a number of familiar phrases: "If ye have faith as a grain of mustard seed"; "without faith it is impossible to please Him"; "all things are possible to him that believeth" (Matthew 17:20; Hebrews 11:6; Mark 9:23). Ellen White said, "Every failure on the part of the children of God is due to their lack of faith," and, "Obedience is the fruit of faith" (*Patriarchs and Prophets*, p. 657; *Steps to Christ*, p. 61). So we have abundant proof that faith is important. And the more important we know faith to be, the more important it is that we understand it aright.

Characteristics of genuine faith

As we have already noticed, faith is trust. It is more than mental assent, or positive thinking. Faith must have an object. It is never an end in itself. It is not something that is worked up. It comes spontaneously, as a result of getting to know Someone who can be trusted. We place our faith in a Person, not in getting answers.

Apparently the disciples of Jesus realized that faith was important, because they came to Jesus one day with a request: "Lord, increase our faith" (Luke 17:5, 6). Here I will paraphrase: Jesus replied, Increase your faith? You don't need more faith. You need to be sure you have the real thing. Faith is not measured in quantity. If you have real faith, you don't need very much. Just the amount of a grain of mustard seed will be enough.

A little faith, if it is genuine, does the impossible. Yet genuine faith will be particularly scarce in the time of the end. Jesus asked, "When the Son of man cometh, shall he find faith on the earth?" (Luke 18:8). By the time of His second coming, the earth will be almost destitute of true faith.

The classic story that illustrates the nature of true faith is found in Matthew 15. Jesus went far out of His way to meet a little "heathen" woman who had a great need. Notice what this experience teaches about the nature of true faith, and compare it to some of our traditional ideas and definitions:

> Then Jesus went thence, and departed into the coasts of Tyre and Sidon. And, behold, a woman of Canaan came out of the same coasts, and cried unto him, saying, Have mercy on me, O Lord, thou son of David; my daughter is grievously vexed with a devil. But he answered her not a word (Matthew 15:21-23).

Here we have a request from one with great faith, yet her request was ignored. The disciples, who were in the habit of judging faith on the basis of answers, concluded immediately that this woman didn't measure up. That's why, when they saw Jesus' apparent refusal, they encouraged Him in His response. They said, "Send her away; for she crieth after us" (verse 23). If you're going to ignore her, go ahead and get rid of her. She's bothering us.

Then Jesus said, "I am not sent but unto the lost sheep of the house of Israel" (verse 24).

The disciples heard Jesus agreeing with them! "I didn't come to help these people. I came to help Israel."

The woman also heard the words of Jesus. But instead of acknowledging His words as an insult, she ignored them and focused on *who He was*. Verse 25 says that she came and "worshiped him."

Have you ever brought a request to God and received no immediate response? What was the first thing the devil tried to tell you? "He won't help you. You're a sinner. His promises are for righteous people—and you don't qualify!"

If your faith is based on positive thinking, you're finished right there! But if you base your faith on whom you know God to be, a Father of love who accepts all who come to Him, you will join this woman at His feet. She had genuine faith!

But before granting her request, Jesus added another insult. He said, "It is not meet [or it is not right] to take the children's bread, and cast it to dogs" (verse 26).

Today we think of dogs as "man's best friend," but back then dogs didn't get good marks. Yet this woman knew something about how dogs were treated, even in her day. The dogs got the crumbs. And here she saw the opening she had been waiting for. If it came from the Master's table, even a crumb would be enough!

At that point, Jesus answered her, "O woman, great is thy faith: be it unto thee even as thou wilt. And her daughter was made whole from that very hour" (verse 28). What a story!

If faith is defined as belief, as taking God at His word, then this woman didn't have faith at all. On the other hand, if faith means clinging to what you know God to be, trusting in His love in spite of appearances, then, as Jesus said, her faith was great.

Faith when things go wrong

One of the tests of true faith is to accept trials, afflictions, and apparently unanswered prayers, and still persist in "worshiping him," as the Canaanite woman did. It's easy to worship Him *after* the answers have been given. But what about *before*?

Does your faith allow for trials and suffering and disappointment? Do you look at the times when trials come to you and ask, "What did I do wrong"? Or have you learned the blessing of trials and heartache? *Is* there a blessing in trouble and affliction? It's easy in our human nature to assume that God's "blessing" means everything is going pleasantly. But God often allows some crisis to come into our lives, not because He enjoys seeing us in a hard place, but in order to get our attention, that we may be drawn nearer to Him in fellowship. He wants to remind us of our dependence upon His grace. And how often we need to be reminded!

Because of our limited understanding, we look on the trials and emergencies of life as negative experiences. But it is through these very means that God invites us into His presence.

While the world is progressing in wickedness, none of us need flatter ourselves that we shall have no difficulties. But it is these very difficulties that bring us into the audience chamber of the Most High. We may seek counsel of One who is infinite in wisdom (*Christ's Object Lessons,* p. 172).

Remember how much trouble the people of Israel had learning this lesson? Remember how every time their supplies got a little low or the enemy threatened them or they found some other cause for discontent, they assumed that God had forsaken them? They didn't understand what He was saying. They misunderstood His invitations to come into His presence! They missed the blessing of trials, and we often do the same thing.

What is your reaction when a crisis comes? Do you rejoice? Or do you rush into God's presence and beg Him to take it away?

> When light shines on our pathway, it is no great thing to be strong in the strength of grace. But to wait patiently in hope when clouds envelop us and all is dark, requires faith and submission which causes our will to be swallowed up in the will of God. We are too quickly discouraged, and earnestly cry for the trial to be removed from us, when we should plead for patience to endure and grace to overcome (*God's Amazing Grace*, p. 114).

So one of the evidences of genuine faith is our willingness to accept the way God leads us to seek Him, to surrender to Him, to come into closer fellowship with Him. Our great need prompts us to come into His presence, even when we have sought Him because of trouble. And the more time we spend in communion with Him the more we will learn to know Him, and the greater will be our faith.

And this brings us to one of the greatest factors in claiming the promises of God's Word: *We cannot base our faith on promises*. We can only base our faith on the Promiser. Human nature shrinks from trial, even though it is good for us. Even Jesus, in His perfect, sinless life, found that He would just as soon skip the hard part. He prayed, "If it be possible, let this cup pass from me." It is human nature to want to avoid suffering. Thus, when we look at the promises God has made, we automatically choose those that fit in with our desires!

But included in the 3,563 Bible promises are some that are pretty negative. If you are inclined to claim Bible promises, try some of these: "In the world ye shall have tribulation" (John 16:33). Is that a promise? Of course it is! What about, "I came not to send peace, but a sword" (Matthew 10:34)? How long has it been since you claimed that one? We are much quicker to claim the other kind of promises, aren't we? We're like foolish children who, left to themselves, would major in candy and ice-cream, and minor in vegetables!

God's 3,563 Bible promises are not every one for us, at this time, and under these circumstances. There's nothing wrong with claiming promises. The problem comes when we try to claim the answers we want or expect.

During the Dark Ages two men, Huss and Jerome, were burned at the stake. They weren't lacking in faith—in fact, they died for their faith. Now there's a good promise for people like that: "When thou walkest through the fire, thou shalt not be burned; neither shall the flame kindle upon thee" (Isaiah 43:2). Should Huss and Jerome have claimed that promise and saved themselves from the flames?

Genuine faith trusts God enough to trust Him with the flames! Look at the three Hebrew worthies in the fiery furnace. God chose to deliver them, not *from* the fire, but *in* the fire. But they didn't know ahead of time what God would choose. They only knew that they could trust Him to make the right choice. Read their words:

O Nebuchadnezzar, we are not careful to answer thee in this matter. If it be so, our God whom we serve is able to deliver us from the burning fiery furnace, and he will deliver us out of thine hand, O king. *But if not*, be it known unto thee, O king, that we will not serve thy gods, nor worship the golden image which thou hast set up (Daniel 3:16-18, emphasis supplied).

Don't forget the "others"

In our understanding of faith and how it relates to Bible promises, we must never forget the "others." Have you read about the "others" lately? The "others" had plenty of faith, and the right kind of faith, as well. They are listed in the "faith chapter"—Hebrews 11.

After naming Bible heroes like Noah, Abraham, Moses, and Gideon, "who through faith subdued kingdoms, wrought righteousness, obtained promises" (verse 33), the author of Hebrews goes on to tell about the "others":

And others had trial of cruel mockings and scourgings, yea, moreover of bonds and imprisonment: they were stoned, they were sawn asunder, were tempted, were slain with the sword: they wandered about in sheepskins and goatskins; being destitute, afflicted, tormented; (of whom the world was not worthy:) they wandered in deserts, and in mountains, and in dens and caves of the earth. And these all, having obtained a good report through faith, *received not the promise* (verses 36-39, emphasis supplied).

Do you like the "others"? Would you like to join them? Only one kind of faith can qualify you to join the "others" club: the faith that trusts in a God of love because of a personal experience and relationship with Him. It is faith that looks to a Person, not to the results of a particular request. All God's heroes had that kind of faith, because they did not necessarily know in advance whether they belonged to the "others" club or not. It required the same faith for Shadrach, Meshach, and Abednego to face the flames as it did for Huss and Jerome. It was the time the had already spent in getting to know God for themselves, the time they had already spent on their knees and in communion with Him, that gave them the faith and trust to go through the fire. The results of being in the fire were beside the point.

Have faith, doubt not

In Matthew 21 we find the story of the cursing of the fig tree. The disciples, for some reason, were greatly intrigued by this miracle of Jesus. You might think that, having seen sight restored to the blind, the dead raised to life, and the stormy sea made calm, one withered fig tree would hardly excite comment or notice. But the Bible says that when the disciples saw the withered fig tree they "marvelled"! Perhaps they were more accustomed to cursing things! After all, they knew how to "call down fire" on the Samaritans.

Whatever the reason, in this small miracle Jesus really got

their attention. In response to their amazement, He said:

> Verily I say unto you, If ye have faith, and *doubt not*, ye shall not only do this which is done to the fig tree, but also if ye shall say unto this mountain, Be thou removed, and be thou cast into the sea; it shall be done. And all things, whatsoever ye shall ask in prayer, believing, ye shall receive (Matthew 21:21, 22, emphasis supplied).

Have you ever remembered this verse and brought some request to God and tried really hard not to doubt? Maybe you joined the little girl with the umbrella, trying somehow to prove that you *really* believed your prayers would be answered.

How do Christians have faith, and "doubt not"?

Unless you are given a special, on-the-spot revelation of God's will in a particular instance, as Peter and John apparently received at the Gate Beautiful (see Acts 3:1-10), you will inevitably have your doubts as to *what* God's response might be. The three Hebrew worthies did, as we noticed. Otherwise, they would not have added, "But if not. . . ." But what you don't doubt, when you have true faith, is *Him*. If you have faith and doubt *Him* not, you will receive His answers to your prayers.

So, once again, we end in the same place: relationship with God. The only way to doubt *Him* not is to know Him. The only way to know *Him* is to spend time with Him, personal time in prayer and in the study of His Word. It's OK to doubt the promises—if by that you mean that you question your own understanding and interpretation of exactly how His promises are going to be fulfilled in your life. You may have no advance warning about whether you will spend the night in the lions' den with Daniel or be eaten by the lions in the Roman arena! But if you know and trust His love, and determine to continue trusting Him regardless of what happens, then you will have the faith that doubts Him not, though pressed by many a foe.

Chapter 10
Prayer for Healing

My wife and I have three children: a boy and two girls. Our second-born was a girl. Lynn apparently had a normal birth and was a happy, active baby. She grew to be a beautiful child, blond and blue-eyed. Nothing in her appearance suggested that she was handicapped. We knew she was "hyper," and we also knew that she seemed somewhat slower than our son, but we thought that was just her way.

About the time that Lynn was ready to begin school, my wife took her to a pediatrician for her preschool examination. He pondered over her a little longer than usual and suggested some further tests. Eventually he diagnosed Lynn as having a recessive gene disorder called PKU (*phenylketonuria*), which causes brain damage. In some cases, the child ends up hardly more than a vegetable. In other cases, such as our daughter's, the damage is less severe.

They told us that the condition is caused by a recessive gene which is carried by one out of every seventy people. Both parents must carry the gene in order for a child to have this disorder, and then an average of one out of four of their children will be affected. Our daughter was one of those four.

The experts predicted that Lynn would probably do well to become literate. We began to learn how her life would be different—and how all of our lives would be different—because of the damage to her brain.

Special education
We discovered that Lynn could not attend church school, for the church school had no facilities for special education. She

would have to attend a special school for handicapped children. One of the hardest things my wife and I have ever had to do was to drive away and leave her there, that first day of school. It didn't take long to learn the facts and statistics about our daughter's condition, but *accepting* her handicap was an entirely different matter. Most of her classmates had handicaps that were obvious at a glance, but Lynn looked as normal and as beautiful as ever. Every day that we took her to school it was a wrenching reminder of our pain. Day after day I would leave her at school and then cry on the way home as I realized anew the difficulties she faced in her future life.

The pain was underlined through the years, as I watched Lynn struggle with simple tasks, such as learning to tell time. It took *years*. Even as a teenager, she still found telling time confusing. By then Lynn had grasped the basic hours and half hours, but we would still overhear when some friend would say, "I'll come by to pick you up at a quarter to four," and she would ask, "Is that *before* four or *after*?"

Mathematics was particularly a mystery. Sometimes I have pictured heaven and what it might be like for her. In my imagination I see crippled children running through the grass. I see the blind children gazing in wonder at the beauty of the flowers. I see those who have become bent and twisted with arthritis now standing straight and tall and flexing their fingers painlessly for the first time in years. And then I hear Lynn reciting her multiplication tables. They had better have multiplication tables up there! She tried so hard and for so long while here on this earth, and with such little success.

Disciplining handicapped children is a perpetual problem. It becomes almost impossible to distinguish between the times when they simply do not understand, and the times when they are disobedient or rebellious. The first few weeks after we learned of Lynn's handicap, we found it impossible to discipline her at all. We were consumed with guilt, wondering how many times we had punished her in the past when she really had not understood why or what was expected of her. It was our eight-year-old boy who brought us up short by saying,

"Since you found out Lynn is sick, she can do anything she wants and never gets punished."

When a child is handicapped, the entire family is handicapped. As our daughter grew older, we found ourselves withdrawing from social life as much as possible. People expect more of the preacher's kids anyway.

The stress in a home with a handicapped child is seldom understood unless you have experienced it. It becomes too easy to focus on the needs of the handicapped child and forget that everyone in the family has needs that should be met. It is a temptation to expect all of the family members to cater to the one.

As parents, we had to remember again and again that we had three children, not just one. Just because one was handicapped did not guarantee that she was always in the right when there were disagreements. Just because she was handicapped didn't mean she should always have her own way— even for *her* sake. But understanding that in theory is one thing. It was quite another thing to be able to judge calmly when the children were at each other's throats and tempers were high. It was so much easier just to discipline the "normal" children and let the other one go free.

My wife carried the greater part of the burden. I had the escape of work outside the home, but she was faced with the constant strain on her nerves, the constant groping in the dark and seeking wisdom for the right way to relate to our children.

A mother's challenge is all the greater with a child who is brain damaged, whose understanding is so limited, and for whom so many of the rules about child rearing seem not to apply. In addition to that, the PKU condition is known for producing hyperactive children. The sheer physical energy of such a child is at times almost unbearable.

Our son, just two years older, has been understanding and protective. I remember one time when they were riding their bicycles—and we were delighted when Lynn learned to ride her bike. They had been out riding together, and a group of kids on the corner who knew that she was in "special ed" at school, called Lynn an M-R. My son got off his bicycle and went over and beat up on the whole bunch of them! For some reason, I was very happy about that. I never felt any remorse at all. That's just a sample of some of the feelings that can come to the surface in this kind of thing.

One of the things I began to notice about this daughter was her prayers. Children often get into routine prayers. My brother and I prayed for years, every night, "Help us not to have bad dreams, help us not to think about war, and help the devil not to jump in the window."

But as I listened to Lynn's prayers, there was something different. I could not explain it, but perhaps the explanation lies in the words of Paul, after he had three times entreated God to remove his handicap. God's answer came: "My grace is sufficient for thee: for my strength is made perfect in weakness" (2 Corinthians 12:9).

This answer can still ring out today for those who struggle with some extra weakness. It became true for our daughter that God's strength was made perfect in her life in a special way. While other boys and girls were praying, "Bless the missionaries and the colporteurs," Lynn would pour out her heart to God, kneeling there beside her bed at night, speaking to Him warmly and easily, as to a friend.

The year Lynn was sixteen years old her brother, who worked at summer camps every summer, encouraged her to try for a summer camp position. This turned out to be an exciting adventure for her, as she helped out in the kitchen at camp. She made friends with some of the other staff who were genuine Christians, and during the summer Lynn began to feel the tug of the Holy Spirit on her heart in a special way. She experienced what to this day I have never doubted was genuine conversion.

Perhaps we don't always value the significance of the conversion experience, but there is no way to be a Christian without it, is there? There's no way. That's biblical! It might be tempting to think that this sort of experience would be unnecessary for the mentally handicapped, but not so. And once the miracle of conversion had happened, the difference was impossible to miss. Since the time of her conversion, Jesus has been our daughter's number one priority, and it never changes. I thank God for that every day.

Lynn wanted to be baptized, but she was too nervous to go in front of everybody at church. So we had a group of friends together one Sabbath afternoon at an outdoor swimming pool in a backyard, and had a baptismal service just for her, complete with singing and all the rest of it. She was thrilled about that.

And so the years went by. Most of our moves or transfers in the ministry were influenced strongly by Lynn's needs at the time. It seemed things would go along somewhat smoothly for a time, and then we would again reach an impasse in terms of her education or some other need. Then the way would open for some new solution or opportunity for her, and we would move again. We learned not to try to plan too far ahead, but to take things a little at a time, trusting God to open new possibilities when each present situation began coming to a close.

Prayer for healing

From almost the very beginning, the question was there: Should we follow the Bible suggestion and call together a group to pray for Lynn and anoint her? If we did, would God heal her?

The thought persisted, often on the back burner, for years. During those years, my understanding of healing was basically that you could ask God to bring healing, and if you had great faith and great righteousness, He might be moved to grant your request. But I didn't think I could qualify! So every time the question came up, I looked for reasons to put off asking, hoping that farther down the road I would finally be ready to bring this request to God—this request that was the closest to my heart.

Very early in my ministry, even before our children were born, I had been called with several others to the bedside of a dying man to anoint him. After the prayer I looked around the room to see who would be the one with enough faith to take him by the hand and say, "In the name of Jesus, rise and walk." But they were all looking at me, and I didn't have enough faith to do it! I mumbled a few words about how we have to accept God's will, and sometimes He says Yes, and sometimes No, and sometimes Wait; and I beat a hasty retreat.

A few days later the man died. I felt that I had killed him! I had killed him because I didn't have enough faith, or enough righteousness, to make it happen. The memory of that experience stayed with me. I wasn't about to make the same mistake with my own daughter and be responsible for causing her more years of pain. So we waited.

The subject of faith became of vital importance to me. The subject of righteousness became equally absorbing. What was faith? What was righteousness? How were they obtained? An interest that might have been soon forgotten was kept front and center in my attention because of the need of one little girl whose sorrows tore at my heart.

The *theory* of righteousness by faith began to come clear, but the experience followed slowly. I wondered, Is it possible that we can gain *salvation* through faith alone, but that when it comes to God's special blessings it's different. Perhaps it is necessary to be just about ready for translation before God could trust us with special blessings such as healing. So we waited.

As I would be called upon in my duties as a minister to pray for and anoint someone, I began to notice that God operated in strange ways. We would gather to pray for some saint in the church, someone who appeared outwardly at least to be deeply committed and mature in his Christian life, but no healing would occur.

Then one night I was called to the bedside of a backslider who lay dying in a nearby hospital. He had lived his life apart from God, had been involved in many sinful things, yet now he was asking for prayer—and I didn't even request that he be healed. I only asked for pardon and acceptance in his behalf. There were no "elders" gathered together, no oil—nothing. And he was healed on the spot!

On another occasion there was an anointing service for one

of the women in the church who was in need of healing, and our Lynn was present. The manifestation of the power of God seemed particulary evident, and the woman was healed.

Afterwards Lynn came and asked, "Daddy, why can't you pray for me like that and have God heal me?"

Would you like to have had the job of answering that one for her? Let me tell you, it was tough! Why, of course we could pray for her! But the thought terrified me. *I wasn't righteous enough yet. I didn't have enough faith,* and there were some very real limits as to how much longer we could keep postponing the decision to ask.

Lynn kept bringing the same question, again and again. "Why can't we ask God to heal me?"

"We can. And we will someday."

"When?"

So I gave her a book to read. Lynn had already been reading the copy of the children's Bible we had gotten for her. She loved to read the stories of Jesus. She understood the stories of Jesus. She love to read about how He healed the people who came to Him. But now I gave her a book on the subject of healing. It was way beyond what she could understand. After working away at it for a time, Lynn brought it back to me and said, "Dad, Jesus didn't make people read books before they were healed!"

She kept after us. She could be very persistent! She didn't demand, but she kept reminding us in every way she could think of. Our family was invited to the Oregon campmeeting about this time. On Sabbath they had a baptism, and the girl who was being baptized told a little bit about her life story, which included having been healed from a long-standing physical problem. Lynn was in the audience. The next day as we were driving toward home she said, "Dad, did you notice that girl who was baptized yesterday?"

"Yes."

"Wasn't that neat that Jesus healed her? I liked that part."

She was ready. But I wasn't. And I was beginning to fear that I would never be ready. Already Lynn was more than twenty years old. Of what value would it be to her to be healed when she was sixty or ninety? If she were to be healed, the time was now, while her life was still ahead of her. We couldn't wait much longer.

So I was faced with a tough decision. Should I refuse to pray for the healing of my own daughter? Or should I go ahead, and take the chance of living the rest of my life knowing that God might have healed her had I been righteous enough and had enough faith? Which should it be?

Good news about healing!

With this background from personal experience, let's get right into the study of the subject of healing. If you take a careful look at everything the Bible says on the subject, including the case histories that are recorded, you will find that there is good news!

There are a least thirty-five cases of healing in the Bible, and the indexed Spirit of Prophecy writings give details about twenty-two that took place during the early days of our church. Let's do a question-and-answer survey of the case histories, noting similarities and contrasts and then try to reach some conclusions.

Who was healed? Men, women, boys, and girls. Young and old. Slaves and common people. Captains and kings. The righteous and the wicked. God's people and the heathen. The blind and lepers and paralytics and those who were demon-possessed. In several cases, those who were healed were suffering under the judgments of God on account of their sin. An example of this would be the children of Israel who were bitten by the fiery serpents in the wilderness.

So who was healed? In a word: everybody! All sorts of people were healed.

How long had they been afflicted? For some, such as the child of the widow in Elijah's time (1 Kings 17:8-24), or the young man who fell asleep in the window during the sermon (Acts 20:8-12), the healing came almost immediately following the onset of the problem—within a few minutes, by the end of the day at most. At the other end of the scale, the blind man in John 9:1-7 had been blind from birth (though we are not told his exact age), and the man by the Pool of Bethesda had been crippled for thirty-eight years (John 5:1-15).

What was the disease? The disease was always something serious! We could take quite a bit of time listing the various diseases: leprosy, blindness, sunstroke, epilepsy, and so on. But when you look at the case histories of healing, one fact stands out: These people were in desperate need. Their diseases were not readily cured by any natural or medical means available at the time. There is no record of anyone being healed, for instance, of a common cold or of a hangnail.

What was the spiritual condition of the individual who was healed? In most cases, not good! Heathen kings, rebellious church members, sinners who were suffering from the results of their own evil lives, those possessed with demons, Philistines and harlots and murderers—all found the mercy of God waiting to bring relief. There is the story, for instance, of a wicked king by the name of Jeroboam. God sent a prophet to warn him from his evil way, and Jeroboam was so angered by the warning that he "put forth his hand from the altar, saying, Lay hold on him."

His arm dried up, so that he could not withdraw it again. The altar was rent, and ashes poured forth.

Jeroboam said to the prophet he had just tried to harm, "Pray for me, that I will be healed."

The man of God prayed, and Jeroboam was healed. On the journey home, the "man of God" disobeyed God's instructions that he take neither food nor drink until he had returned home—and he was eaten by a lion! (see 1 Kings 13).

Do you like that story? Or does it worry you that God is so generous with His miracles of healing? One thing is certain. If you take a careful look at each case history in the Bible, you will have a hard time insisting that the healing is reserved for only the very righteous.

Perhaps we should add here that there are also instances in which the righteous were healed! They don't have a corner on the market, but they *are* included.

Was there an intercessor involved? In many instances, yes. Often the request for healing was presented by an intercessor.

But in other cases, the one seeking the healing asked in his own behalf.

What was the spiritual position of the intercessor? Often the intercessor was close to God. However, there is an interesting story that comes from the early days of the Advent movement, when a certain minister was called to pray for a woman who was sick. The lady is described as "a true disciple of Christ," but the minister who took the role of intercessor is described as vile, corrupt, and taking all the glory to himself. Ellen White comments that "her faith was that she should be healed," but his prayers were dark, misty, and "fell downward." Yet she was healed, in spite of his lack of faith (see *Selected Messages*, bk. 2, p. 347).

What was the result of the request for healing? The overwhelming majority of answers to requests for healing were Yes. Paul is one of the few exceptions. He prayed three times for the thorn in his flesh to be removed, and was told No each time. Yet even Paul received a definite answer. He could look back to the specific time, after his third request, when God said No: "My grace is sufficient for you" (2 Corinthians 12: 9, NIV). He wasn't left wondering whether God had heard his prayer.

How long did the healing take? Usually the answer came immediately. There was a short delay in some cases, such as for the Syrophoenician woman or for the blind man who was sent to wash the mud from his eyes in the Pool of Siloam. Lazarus's healing was delayed by four days—which he spent in the tomb! But more often than not, the request was granted immediately.

What about the faith of the person healed, or of the intercessor? In five or six instances Jesus commented on the faith of the ones who had come seeking His help. However, as in the case of the ten lepers, nine had no faith—and less gratitude. Their hearts were untouched by the mercy of God (see *The Ministry of Healing*, page 233). Yet they were healed. Simon the Pharisee was healed *before* accepting Jesus as Saviour. The man at the Pool of Bethesda had so little faith that he never requested healing—and when Jesus offered to make him whole, he even despaired of being carried down the steps the next time the water would be troubled (see John 5:1-9).

It's almost as if it was a bonus when Jesus had the privilege of healing someone who had great faith, and He commented on it by saying, "My, that's sure nice faith you have!" But He did not refuse help to those whose faith was weak.

Ellen White comments about the nobleman who came to Jesus to ask that his son be healed. He doubted and he questioned, "Yet the nobleman had a degree of faith; for he had come to ask what seemed to him the most precious of all blessings" (*The Desire of Ages*, p. 198). Think about that for a moment. Do you have to have some tremendous amount of faith to get started? No, apparently it's enough if you have just enough to come and ask. And where that is not enough, you can join the nobleman in discovering that the grace of God can somehow supply whatever else is needed. "The Saviour cannot withdraw from the soul that clings to Him, pleading its great need" (*ibid.*). We can pray with the father of the demon-possessed boy at the foot of the mountain, "Lord, I believe; help *thou* mine unbelief" (Mark 9:24, emphasis supplied). And whatever extra is needed in the faith department will be provided.

Great need and no merit

When you study carefully the information we have been given about healing, you can see two common threads running throughout. First, those who were healed were in great need of healing, and second, they had nothing which would qualify them for God's help. Does that sound like it would be hard for you to qualify? If you have a great need, and if you have just enough faith to come, saying, "In my hand no price I bring, simply to Thy cross I cling," then you have fulfilled the conditions. The mercy of God is great enough to take care of the rest.

For the one who seeks healing of himself, or for one who finds himself an intercessor for the needs of another, these inspired case studies can provide encouragement and counsel. It is not the amount of faith *or* righteousness that makes the difference. Rather, it is the realization of helplessness and unworthiness that God values. When you realize this good news, you can take your eyes off of yourself and direct them to the Great Physician, for it is never our merits, but always the merits of Jesus, that enable us to receive any of God's gifts and blessings.

We can understand that sometimes God says No to those who are the *most* righteous and the most filled with genuine faith, as in the case of Paul. This delivers us from discouragement, guilt, and despair if God does not see fit to grant our particular request for healing. And the fact that He has sometimes said Yes to those who were unrighteous and doubting will protect us from spiritual pride, from taking the glory and the credit to ourselves when He grants our request. When God gives us what we ask, it is always because of *His* goodness, never because of ours.

And so we are free at any time to bring to Him the desires of our hearts, with the argument of our great need and His great mercy. If we have learned to love and trust Him through our personal relationship with Him *before* tragedy strikes, then, regardless of the outcome, we will continue to walk with Him.

Often the question is asked, "Why doesn't God heal everybody who asks to be healed? When Jesus was here on this earth, no one who came to Him was ever refused. Why is it different today?"

Ellen White mentions three times when Jesus could not heal even though He wanted to. The first is the story of the man at the Pool of Bethesda. It was early in His ministry. Not for long would He be able to walk unnoticed among the crowds in Jerusalem. But on this Sabbath day, coming to the pool, He looked with compassion on the suffering and helpless ones who were there. "He longed to exercise His healing power, and make every sufferer whole" (*The Desire of Ages*, p. 201). But He couldn't. If you read the story, you will find the reason: He couldn't bring healing without interfering with His mission to save the world. Even the case of the one man whom Jesus somehow could not pass by was enough to cause such a tumult that if the Jews had been left to their own choice, they would have put Him to death immediately. If He had healed them all, His greater work would have been interrupted. That's one reason why Jesus sometimes has to say No.

The second time Jesus was unable to heal, even though He would have wanted to is found in the story of the leper who came to Him for cleansing. Jesus said two things to him after restoring him to health: "Go show yourself to the priests," and "Don't tell anybody!"

The leper went along with the first part, but ignored the second. Ellen White says that "it would indeed have been impossible to conceal it, but the leper published the matter abroad" (*The Desire of Ages*, p. 265). As a result, the curious crowd came in such great numbers that Jesus was forced for a time to withdraw from His work. Then comes this significant paragraph:

Every act of Christ's ministry was far-reaching in its purpose. It comprehended more than appeared in the act itself. So in the case of the leper. While Jesus ministered to all who came unto Him, He yearned to bless those who came not. While He drew publicans, the heathen, and the Samaritans, He longed to reach the priests and teachers who were shut in by prejudice and tradition. He left untried no means by which they might be reached.

Is the principle here that Jesus picks favorites, that He'll heal some but not others? No. The issue at stake is that Jesus does *not* have favorites, and sometimes He has to say No to His friends in order to reach those who are His enemies!

That might seem unfair to His friends. If Jesus sometimes has to refuse those who come to Him in order to be free to reach those who do not come, then that's unfair to the ones who come—except for one thing: Since Jesus has all wisdom and power at His command, He has an alternate route that takes away the sting of unfairness. He does have an alternative: "If He sees it best not to grant their desires He will counterbalance the refusal by giving them tokens of his love" (*The Ministry of Healing*, p. 473).

He did it with John the Baptist. "Though no miraculous deliverance was granted John, he was not forsaken. He had always the companionship of heavenly angels" (*The Desire of Ages*, p. 224). Then follows this classic paragraph:

> God never leads His children otherwise than they would choose to be led, if they could see the end from the beginning, and discern the glory of the purpose which they are fulfilling as co-workers with Him. Not Enoch, who was translated to heaven, not Elijah, who ascended in a chariot of fire, was greater or more honored than John the Baptist, who perished alone in the dungeon. "Unto you is given in the behalf of Christ, not only to believe on Him, but also to suffer for His sake." Philippians 1:29. And of all the gifts that Heaven can bestow upon men, fellowship with Christ in His sufferings is the most weighty trust and the highest honor.

Another factor comes to light in the story of the healing of the leper. "Many of the lepers would not so use the gift of health as to make it a blessing to themselves or to others" (*The Desire of Ages*, p. 264). God apparently sees in some cases that the person is better off as he is! You might be tempted to read this about the lepers and say, "That's right, they weren't righteous enough to be healed." But even God's own children may not be helped by healing. Remember Hezekiah, who pleaded for an extension to his life? He was like a child who wanted to stay up past his bedtime! God granted the request, perhaps as an object lesson for the rest of us, but the king would have been better off to go to sleep the first time. He begged to stay up, and the Father permitted it: but it did not turn out to be the blessing that Hezekiah had hoped for.

One thing we can count on: When we come to God with our

special requests, He will either give us that for which we have asked, or He will give us something better. "Even when called upon to surrender those things which in themselves are good, we may be sure that God is thus working out for us some higher good. . . . We shall see that our seemingly unanswered prayers and disappointed hopes have been among our greatest blessings" (*The Ministry of Healing*, pp. 473, 474).

The third time Jesus was unable to heal, even though He would have wanted to, happened when He visited His hometown of Nazareth. The reason given? "*Because of their unbelief*, the Saviour could not work many miracles among them. Only a few hearts were open to His blessing, and reluctantly He departed, never to return" (*The Desire of Ages*, p. 241, emphasis supplied).

Here it might be easy to miss the point if you are not sure of your definition for faith. Did the people of Nazareth disbelieve that Jesus had the power to heal? No, they had heard the reports from far and wide. It wasn't His ability as a Healer that they did not believe. It was who He was. The unbelief was in *Him*, not in what He might *do*. Because of their unbelief in Him, they refused to enter into relationship with Him. They did not seek His blessing. That's why He was unable to work for them as He longed to do. Jesus is not pushy. He does not force His blessings on anyone. The people of Nazareth wanted nothing to do with Him, and He reluctantly accepted their choice.

But this should never be confused with God's response to His children who, though weak and faltering, still long to be His children. Here are encouraging words for every one who seeks Him:

> Trust in the Lord with all your heart, and He will never betray your trust. If you will ask help of God you need not ask in vain. In order to encourage us to have confidence and trust He comes near us by His holy Word and Spirit, and seeks in a thousand ways to win our confidence. But in nothing does He take more delight than in receiving the weak who come to Him for strength. If

we will find heart and voice to pray, He will be sure to find an ear to hear and an arm to save.

There is not a single instance in which God has hidden His face from the supplication of His people. When every other resource failed He was a present help in every emergency. God bless you, poor, stricken, wounded soul. Cling to His hand; hold fast. He will take you, your children, and all your griefs and burdens if you will only cast them all upon Him (*This Day With God,* p. 194).

So while there may be good reasons for God to refuse your most earnest request, He will always meet your need in the way He sees is best. Sometimes He delivers *from* affliction, while at other times He brings deliverance *through* affliction. But we can always depend on Him to respond to those who seek Him.

The rest of the story

Once we began to understand more clearly the issues at stake in prayer for healing, my wife and I were no longer afraid to bring Lynn to Jesus with this special request. Oh, we certainly had a preference! Never have we wanted anything as much as we wanted healing for our daughter! But the fear was gone. We felt safe in asking.

It seemed important to share some of these truths with Lynn, in order that she be fully prepared for God's response, whatever it might be. But her childlike faith had been ready long ago! She said calmly, "It's OK if God doesn't heal me. I know it won't be my fault. I can accept it if it is His will, and I can wait till He comes. But I still want to *ask* Him."

So we set a date, gathered together with some close friends and other family members, and brought this request before the Lord. We asked that God would bring healing if it was His will. The Spirit of God was very close, and it was a blessed experience. There were no bolts of lightning, no visiting angels, no fire from heaven. However, one thing particularly impressed my son. It was cloudy all that day—but the sun broke through for just a few moments during the prayer, and during the anointing it shone through the window right on Lynn, bathing her in light. We saw this as a special communication from heaven! After the service was over, our friends went on their way and we began watching, trying to determine whether our request had been denied. We wondered how soon we would know for sure.

God in His love did not leave us wondering for long. Within just a day or two, through various means, He let us know that the answer was No. Along with His answer He gave us peace that He would stay with us and give us wisdom and courage to go forward.

There is a blessing in knowing that with the answer, there came an acceptance that we had never known before. There was a feeling of completion—a sense of being settled. We were freed to focus more on trying to discover the things Lynn *could* do, instead of noticing quite so much the things she could not do.

In the process of seeking every possible skill that she could make use of, we remembered how she had always loved older people. Whenever I took her with me to visit the nursing home on a Sabbath afternoon, Lynn's usual shyness would disappear. As she saw others who were weaker than she, suddenly she would blossom. Down the hall she would go, saying, "See you later, Dad." When I was ready to leave, I would have to pull her away!

We were able to arrange for her to take the nurses' aide course at a nearby nursing home. Lynn went through the class three times before she finished—but she finished! And then there was her driver's license. God was able to say Yes about the driver's license—and I know He must have rejoiced as much as we did!

The driver's license

Lynn longed to be able to drive a car. We didn't expect her ever to be ready to take the car out across the country by herself, or to tackle downtown Los Angeles during rush hour. But it did seem that she ought to be able to drive herself back and forth on the quiet streets of our small town.

The first hurdle was the driver's training manual—the rules of the road for California. It was a hard book! She studied and studied in an effort to understand the traffic laws. Finally one day we took her down to try the written test.

They called her name and handed her the test, and I had a chance to take a quick look at it before they sent her off to a back room. I went to the front of the building to pray! The test looked impossible. But she passed! In fact, she told me later about some of the questions that she knew the answers to that I didn't know! She was so excited about beginning her behind-the-wheel training, and she learned to drive in a relatively short time.

The next major hurdle was the road test. When the time came, I asked several people about the easiest place to take it. We drove to the recommended office of the Department of Motor Vehicles, and suddenly I had a bright idea. Instead of going inside and signing up right away, we parked out in front and waited. The next time an officer brought someone out for a test, we followed them, staying back a little way but watched to see the course they took. It was a hard course. One intersection in particular was absolutely impossible. I couldn't believe it. Five different streets came in from strange angles. The instructor brought the driver in from the right, through a stop sign. Just past the intersection was an overpass, and right after that they made a left turn. The heavy traffic from all directions made it almost impossible for me to drive—let alone her.

When we came to that spot, I said, "Oh my. We're in big trouble." And I was tempted to go home and forget the whole thing.

Then I thought, "Maybe they don't always take this route." So we drove back to the office and followed another instructor. He took the very same course. And I broke out in a hot and cold sweat.

Finally, as Lynn insisted, we went inside and signed her up. I was sure that I hadn't helped things any with all my spying, because now it was almost closing time, and the five o'clock rush hour was beginning. It seemed hopeless.

I watched to see who would be testing her, hoping for a nice, kind-looking officer. Unfortunately, he didn't look that way at all. In fact, he looked rather stern. All of them looked mean that day!

I wanted to ride along, but the officer wouldn't allow it. So Lynn got in, and off they went. I leaned up against the stone wall of the Department of Motor Vehicles, and almost as though I was at the wailing wall in Jerusalem, I began to pray: God, please, do something. Please, send the angels to do something!"

A little while later they pulled up by the curb. Lynn was grinning from ear to ear, and the officer came over and told me that she had passed the test! I almost hugged him! He didn't look stern anymore!

When we got back into the car I said to her, "What happened when you got to that bad intersection?"

"There wasn't a single car there," she said. "Not one. I just drove right on through."

That's one miracle I intend to check on someday. I want to find out how many angels it took to arrange that!

As you would expect of any loving parent, God is absolutely guaranteed to say Yes just as often as He dares! And He shares our joy with us. Lynn has now enjoyed a number of years of safe driving—no accidents, no tickets. Her story isn't over yet, though, because every new year of life brings new challenges. But we know that God will stay with us, and with her, through it all.

Why me? Why her? Why them?

When tragedy strikes, the experts tell us that the first stage is to ask, "Why me?

The second stage, coming soon after, we hope, asks, "Why *her?*" The attention and sympathy moves away from yourself as you begin to realize the impact that the sorrow is having on the one who is dear to you.

Then, as you continue to adjust, you come to the third stage: "Why *them?* Why *all* of them?" For the world is full of hurting people. When you experience hurt for yourself, you suddenly become more aware of the pain of others.

One time I had a disk problem with my back. That's all it took—people began coming out of the woodwork with disk problems! Everybody and his uncle had a disk problem. I just didn't hear about it until I had mine!

Part of God's business is to let us become aware of the pain of others so that we do not become lost in our own hurts, for as we reach out to help others we find help and comfort for ourselves.

One time I was teaching a college class, and a student asked, "If God loved the world so much, why didn't He come Himself? Why did He take the easy way out and send His Son?"

I knew the answer to that one before he finished the sentence! But before I could open my mouth, another student replied, "If you are a loving Father, you would much rather suffer yourself than to watch your child suffer."

I said to him, "You're a father, aren't you?"

And he said, "Yes."

Anyone who has watched a loved one suffer knows. Anyone who loves would rather suffer himself, than to watch the suffering of the one he loves. I cannot tell you how many times I have prayed, "God, please, please let me trade places with her."

But God has given us a gift in this special daughter. He has drawn me closer to Him because of her pain—and because of my pain. I understand a little more about His love because of what I have seen through this part of my life. It gives God and me just one more thing in common—because, you see, He has brain damaged children too. All of us are damaged, born into this world of sin. And many of God's heartaches are the same as mine. I know Him better today, because of her.

My friend Jay Davis sent me an excerpt from a graduation talk he gave which I have prized and which I would like to share:

> There is great interest and excitement these days created by the Olympic games. There is also growing support for a movement called the Special Olympics, a

program that gives those specially challenged—the handicapped—a chance to strive, a chance to feel the thrill of putting their best on the line. They are invited to run, all out, to a friend or family member who calls encouragement from the finish line. No matter if the performance is awkward or clumsy. Everyone who finishes is a winner and is given a prize and hugs and glory.

Every time I witness one of these contests, I choke up because, you see, *I* am handicapped. I have a birth defect. I am a born sinner. And waiting at the finish line of this special race I'm in, reaching out to *me* and calling to me, is my beloved Father, who loves me—why, I don't understand. I'm slow and clumsy and awkward. My limbs won't work the way I want them to. Sometimes I look away from Him and stumble. I get off course and fall down, embarrassed and ashamed. But I have an Elder Brother beside me who helps me when I fall, who holds me up, and who even carries me.

Now, throughout this race, there is a heckler who delights in browbeating me. He keeps telling me there's no use to keep coming to my Father. He says that my Father at the finish line is disgusted with my performance, that I'm just making a spectacle of myself for nothing. However, when I look in the face of my loving Father, He is always there, reaching out to me.

"But I've shamed You," I cry.

He calls back, "Get up. Just keep coming."

And I am beginning to realize that the others in this special race—all with birth defects—are not my competitors at all. *They* are running to *their* Father, just as I am, struggling to finish, because everyone who keeps coming until the end of the race is a winner.

The longer this race continues, the more my attention span lengthens. Distractions grow weaker, and I can see His face more clearly. He *does* want me to get there! This is becoming a glorious race, as He keeps reaching out to me, encouraging me to keep coming to Him, even when I falter.

The day is not far off when each one of us can stumble in our awkwardness across the finish line and lurch into His waiting arms. He'll gather you in, and clasp you in His arms, and you'll know you're a winner—because He kept calling you, and you kept coming to Him. He's there, waiting for you, because He loves you. He really loves you.

Chapter 11
Persistence in Prayer

Perhaps you heard the story of Andy. Andy wanted to share his faith, so he began going around the block once a week, leaving literature at each home. The first week, when he came to one house, he walked up the steps and knocked on the door.

A man came to the door. "Can I help you?"

Andy offered the literature.

The man said, "No thanks; I'm not interested." And he closed the door. Andy stuck the literature in the door handle and went on his way. The next week when Andy reached that particular house, he walked up the steps and knocked on the door.

The man came to the door and shouted at him; "I told you that I'm not interested!" And he slammed the door in Andy's face.

Andy stuck the literature in the door handle and went on around the block.

The third week when Andy reached that particular house, he went up the steps and knocked on the door. The man opened the door, broke a beer bottle over Andy's head, and slammed the door.

Andy stood there for a few moments, holding on to the porch railing, waiting for his head to clear. Then he stuck the literature in the door handle and went on his way.

The following week when Andy reached that house, he went up the stairs and knocked on the door. The man opened the door and shouted, "When are you going to get the message? Are you going to *keep* coming back?"

Andy replied, "Now *you've* got the message!"

The man invited him in! Today the man is an elder in his local church. He was finally won over by Andy's persistence. Andy, whose full name is Andrew Fearing, had plenty of persistence. Perhaps that's one of the reasons why he was so successful as an evangelist!

Persistence is an important ingredient in effective prayer. When we pray, sometimes God answers our prayers immediately. And that's good news! But often He chooses to wait awhile. In fact, He has a habit of waiting until the last minute! So if you are facing a crisis—let's say that within thirty days you will face bankruptcy—you can relax! The answer to your prayer for deliverance very likely won't come for another twenty-nine and a half days!

Delay and waiting have perplexed many of God's children. We are impatient. We humans don't like to wait. The "Now Generation" wasn't invented in our day. Every generation since the beginning of time has been a Now Generation.

Take a look at one of the Old Testament case histories: the story of Saul, the first king of Israel. Saul was an impatient man. Early in his reign, at the end of a battle with the Philistines, he was supposed to meet the prophet Samuel at a certain place. They had an appointment at the end of seven days to offer sacrifices before the Lord, but Samuel was late for the appointment. We have the insight that God purposely arranged the delay. So when Samuel didn't appear right on schedule, Saul went ahead by himself, offering sacrifices that only a priest was allowed to do (see 1 Samuel 13:1-9; *Patriarchs and Prophets,* pp. 617, 618).

We next hear about the impatient Saul when he needed counsel about attacking the Philistines. He wasn't sure whether to go after them or not, so he enquired of the Lord, but the Lord didn't answer him "that day" (see 1 Samuel 14:37). Saul wanted an answer *right away*. He wasn't willing to wait, so he followed his own wisdom instead of persisting in prayer until God's answer came.

Near the close of his life Saul failed the test a third time. Once again, he wanted counsel as to whether to go into battle:

"When Saul enquired of the Lord, the Lord answered him not, neither by dreams, nor by Urim, nor by prophets." Saul didn't wait around, though. Since God was silent, he sought out the witch of Endor. When the witch managed to produce a being that had the appearance of Samuel, and who pretended to be Samuel, his first words betrayed him. He asked, "Why hast thou disquieted me, to bring me up?" That should have been a clue for Saul right there. This was not someone sent from God—he came from the wrong direction!

But Saul said, "God is departed from me, and answereth me no more, neither by prophets, nor by dreams: therefore I have called thee, that thou mayest make known unto me what I shall do" (1 Samuel 28:1-20).

The history of Saul is a sad commentary on one who failed to persist in prayer, waiting for God to give *His* answer. And you remember the end of the story. Saul saw that the battle was against him and, overcome with terror, fell upon his sword, thus ending his own life (see 1 Samuel 31:1-6).

The widow before the unjust judge

Let's go now to a Bible example of one who did it right. She was a widow. Jesus used her to show the importance of persistence:

> He spake a parable unto them to this end, that men ought always to pray, and not to faint; saying, There was in a city a judge, which feared not God, neither regarded man: and there was a widow in that city; and she came unto him, saying, Avenge me of mine adversary. And he would not for a while: but afterward he said within himself, Though I fear not God, nor regard man; yet because this widow troubleth me, I will avenge her, lest by her continual coming she weary me. And the Lord said, Hear what the unjust judge saith. And shall not God avenge his own elect, which cry day and night unto him, though he bear long with them? I tell you that he will avenge them speedily. Nevertheless when the son of man cometh, shall he find faith on the earth? (Luke 18:1-8).

We can emphasize right to begin with that God is *not* like the unjust judge in the parable. The purpose of persistence is not to break down God's unwillingness to give us the things that we need. The parable shows God's personality by contrast. If even an unjust judge can be won over by persistence, how much more a Father of love who is always willing to give to His children.

But do you ever wonder why, since God is so willing to give, He takes so long to answer? The parable says, "He will avenge them speedily," but some of us have discovered that God's definition of the word *speedily* is far different from ours!

The same thing is true about the word *quickly*. In Revelation 3:11 we find the promise, "Behold, I come quickly." Has He come quickly according to your understanding?

In the book *Voyage of the "Dawn Treader"* from the Chronicles of Narnia, C. S. Lewis suggests an interesting question. The lion, Aslan, who is a type of Christ, comes to where the children are staying, lingers for a short while giving them needed counsel, then prepares to leave. He says, "I will see you again soon."

Lucy, one of the children, asks, "Please, Aslan, what do you call *soon?*"

Many of God's children have asked Him that question. God's timetable has often proved different from ours. This is one of the major reasons why it is so important to study persistence in prayer. You'd better understand it, because sooner or later you're going to need it!

Isaiah helps us to understand God's definition of *speedily* and *quickly*: "I foretold the former things long ago, my mouth announced them and I made them known; then suddenly I acted, and they came to pass." "I am the Lord; in its time I will do this swiftly" (Isaiah 48:3; 60:22, NIV).

So the key to understanding apparent delays in God's answers is to understand that while there may appear to be a delay *before* He moves, *when* He moves, watch out—He moves fast! This helps us put together the two phrases from the parable, "though He bear long with them", and, "He will avenge them speedily." Since we are assured of God's love and concern for us, we can also be assured that whatever persistence is necessary in the face of delay, it is for our good.

There is no danger that the Lord will neglect the prayers of His people. The danger is that in temptation and trial they will become discouraged, and fail to persevere in prayer (*Christ's Object Lessons*, p. 175).

What is the purpose of persistence, anyway? If we understand a little more about why persistence is so important, and what God's purpose is in letting us wait so often, perhaps the danger that we will fail to persevere in prayer will be lessened.

The purpose of persistence

Persistence is a discipline. We tend to look at discipline in terms of punishment, but it has a positive side as well. Discipline is the self-control that leads to growth, and even positive self-control can at times be unpleasant—as any student knows! Have you ever had the discipline of studying for a test? It wasn't necessarily fun—but it was good for you, wasn't it? What good is there about persistence?

It leads us to search our own hearts. God is interested in showing us what really makes us tick. We find it easy to deceive ourselves, particularly when things are going smoothly. But when there is a delay in the answer to our prayers, we are motivated to take a closer look at what we really are.

When we make request of Him, He may see that it is necessary for us to search our hearts and repent of sin. Therefore He takes us through test and trial, He brings us through humiliation, that we may see what hinders the working of His Holy Spirit through us (*ibid.*, p. 143).

Through persistence, God can give us a greater blessing than we ask. The nobleman came to Jesus to ask what seemed to him the greatest possible blessing: He wanted his son to be healed. And Jesus wanted his son to be healed too! But Jesus had more than healing to give this man. He delayed the answer to his request, in spite of the temporary discomfort that resulted. The result was a greater blessing both to him and his son, and to his entire household.

We are often led to seek Jesus by the desire for some earthly good; and upon the granting of our request we rest our confidence in His love. The Saviour longs to give us a greater blessing than we ask; and He delays the answer to our request that He may show us the evil of our own hearts, and our deep need of His grace. He desires us to renounce the selfishness that leads us to seek Him. Confessing our helplessness and bitter need, we are to trust ourselves wholly to His love (*The Desire of Ages,* p. 200).

Persistence reveals genuine faith. Persistence tries our faith and reveals whether it is genuine. Do we get unhappy with God if we don't get what we think we need, or what we want, right away? If so, we need to find that out! I used to become very angry with God for waiting until the last minute, but it was good for me! I *needed* to see how quickly I got angry with God when He didn't do what I wanted Him to do. "Often He delays to answer us in order to try our faith" (*Christ's Object Lessons,* p. 145).

Having to wait tests the genuineness of the desire. Waiting is part of life for all of us. We wait for a letter in the mail. We wait for payday. We wait at the stoplights. We wait for appointments with doctors and dentists. We wait in line at the store. Christians also often have to wait in their own unique ways. We are still waiting for Jesus to come. We may be waiting for the fruits of the Spirit to develop in our lives. And we may be waiting for the answer to some prayer.

We tend to view time spent waiting as wasted time, but it is still true that "to wait on God, no time is lost." All down through the ages God's people have waited. At the head of the line was Adam, who waited for more than 900 years for the promised Son to be born. He was still waiting when he died. Noah waited 120 years for the flood to come. Moses waited forty years, forty more years, and finally forty *more* years for the Promised Land. He lay down alone on the top of Mount Nebo, still waiting. Jacob waited seven years for his bride—and then was given the wrong bride! The ten virgins in Jesus' parable waited for the bridegroom. And Hebrews 11:13 talks about a group who waited all of their lives:

> These all died in the faith, not having received the promises, but having seen them afar off, and were persuaded of them, and embraced them, and confessed that they were strangers and pilgrims on the earth.

But when you are waiting for something, you have plenty of time to consider whether you really want it. Have you ever gone into a store to purchase a particular item and waited so long in line that you decided it wasn't worth waiting for? The longer you have to wait, the more sure you have to be that you *really* want the thing for which you wait. "Often He delays to answer us in order to . . . test the genuineness of our desire" (*Christ's Object Lessons,* p. 145).

Persistence increases our desire for the answer. When you focus your attention on a particular desire, and continue to seek for it, your desire increases! It's like waiting for Thanksgiving dinner! The longer you have to wait, the hungrier you get! And the more you appreciate it when it comes time to eat.

> Persistent asking brings the petitioner into a more earnest attitude, and gives him an increased desire to receive the things for which he asks (*ibid.*).

Delay brings us into closer union with Christ. If we accept the discipline of waiting and persist in bringing our prayers before Him, our union with Christ is increased. "The more earnestly and steadfastly we ask, the closer will be our spiritual union with Christ" (*ibid.,* p. 146). Persistence in prayer keeps us in His presence—and the more time we spend in His presence, the more we will become acquainted with Him.

Waiting prepares us to receive the answer when it is given. We may not always be ready to receive the answer at the time we ask. Moses wasn't ready to lead the people of Israel out of Egypt at the end of his first forty years. He thought he was, but God saw that he needed more time. In fact, he needed a second forty years before he was prepared to *begin* the work God has assigned for him.

> Wait on the Lord until he sees that you are ready to receive and appreciate the blessings for which you ask (Ellen G. White, *Review and Herald,* May 30, 1912).

Persistence keeps you from taking God's gifts for granted. It's so easy to take God's gifts for granted. If you doubt that, stop and think for a minute: which of these gifts from God have you thanked Him for within the last twenty-four hours: sunlight, fingernails, rest, water, shoes, indoor plumbing, your guardian angel, blankets, music, and religious freedom? Did you get 100 percent? One thing is certain: if you were particularly thankful for anything on that random list, it is because you were somehow made aware of what it would be like not to have it. It's easy to take things for granted. But when we are allowed to wait, and continue seeking for a particular blessing, we are much less likely to take it for granted.

At the time Elijah prayed for rain on top of Mount Carmel there had been no rain for three and a half years. That would already seem long enough! But by the time he had prayed seven times for the rain to begin, it was even more impossible for him to take God's response for granted. Commenting on this experience, Ellen White said:

> God does not always answer our prayers the first time we call upon Him; for should He do this, we might take it for granted that we had a right to all the blessings and favors He bestowed upon us. Instead of searching our hearts to see if any evil was entertained by us, any sin indulged, we should become careless, and fail to realize our dependence upon Him, and our need of His help

(Ellen G. White Comments, *SDA Bible Commentary,* vol. 2, p. 1035).

Waiting can keep you from taking the glory for what God has done. Elijah again, there on Mount Carmel: he prayed for fire, and the fire came instantly. Now the danger was that he should think it had somehow been his work instead of God's, so God put him "on hold" while he prayed for rain.

Elijah humbled himself until he was in a condition where he would not take the glory to himself. This is the condition upon which the Lord hears prayer, for then we shall give the praise to Him. . . .

As he searched his heart, he seemed to be less and less, both in his own estimation and in the sight of God. It seemed to him that he was nothing, and that God was everything; and when he reached that point of renouncing self, while he clung to the Saviour as his only strength and righteousness, the answer came (*ibid.*).

The delay makes God's interference more marked. If every answer to prayer came quickly and easily, we might conclude that it would have happened anyway. But when we reach an impasse, when we come to the end of our own resources, we will more easily recognize His hand in bringing us out on the other side.

From age to age the Lord has made known the manner of His working. When a crisis has come, He has revealed Himself, and has interposed to hinder the working out of Satan's plans. With nations, with families, and with individuals, He has often permitted matters to come to a crisis, that His interference might become marked. Then He has made manifest that there is a God in Israel who will maintain His law and vindicate His people (*Christ's Object Lessons,* p. 178).

Not only does the delay to the point of crisis make God's

working more clear to our own hearts, but it also is a testimony to others who are watching. You may not be the one who needs this painful delay, but God can use it to get the attention of those around you. Are you willing for God to use you in that way?

From your own experience you may be able to add to these ten points reasons you have discovered why persistence can be a blessing. Even though it may at times seem unpleasant, persistence is a necessary part of our discipline as children of the King.

Why do we give up so easily?

Since persistence in prayer is so necessary, and is good for us for so many different reasons, why do we find it so hard? There are at least three reasons.

First, we have more faith in what we can do for ourselves than in what God can do for us. That was Abraham's problem. He put his faith in what he was able to work out with Hagar instead of waiting for God to give him Isaac.

Second, we often fail to realize our own need. We ask halfheartedly, perhaps because we think it is expected, but we are not really aware of how helpless we are apart from Him. We don't realize how desperately we need His power in our lives. And so we are content to give up the seeking.

And third, we fail to realize God's willingness to give. It's easy when there is a delay to forget that God is more willing to give good things to us than we are willing to give to our children. We interpret the delay as a lack of concern on His part, and thus fail to persevere.

But persistence is not something that we manufacture for ourselves. Persistence is a gift! (see *Christ's Object Lessons*, p. 175). "It was Christ who gave the pleading widow courage and determination before the judge." So if you need persistence, don't try to work it up for yourself. He will give you the persistence you need as you continue in relationship with Him.

One of the ways He gives persistence is through pain. When

you are in pain, no one has to remind you to continue seeking relief! It comes naturally and spontaneously! Luke records that, "being in an agony he [Jesus] prayed more earnestly" (Luke 22:44). Have you discovered that there are enough bumps and bruises living in this world of sin that we have a constant reminder of our need for God? If only we will accept the discipline and keep coming to Him!

How long should we persist? The Syrophoenician woman asked three times and got an answer. The answer was Yes. Paul also asked three times and got an answer. The answer was No. But he got an answer! How long should we keep praying? Until we get a response from God. It's that simple.

Moses prayed to enter the Promised Land until God told him to stop asking. We often bring a request to God and assume that the answer is No unless we are shown otherwise. But the Bible examples teach us that we should expect the answer to be Yes, and continue pleading until we are either told to stop or we receive the blessing. You don't stop just because you don't see results. You don't stop even when God *apparently* says No (see Exodus 32). You don't stop until God tells you to stop!

It is not a lack of faith to continue pressing your case. There is no need to feel guilty for not letting go. "If the answer is deferred, it is because God desires us to show a holy boldness in claiming the pledged word of God" (*In Heavenly Places,* p. 74).

When with earnestness and intensity we breathe a prayer in the name of Christ, there is in that very intensity a pledge from God that He is about to answer our prayer "exceedingly abundantly above all that we ask or think" (*ibid.,* p. 80).

God has invited us to ask. He encourages our prayers. He wants us to keep on asking in order that we may receive; to keep on seeking that we may find; and to keep on knocking that the door may be opened unto us (see Matthew 7:7).

Chapter 12
When God Speaks

God is a good listener! Have you discovered that yet? He patiently allows us to do most of the talking, even though He's heard it all before! He knows what we are going to say before we say it. There isn't a single thing we can tell Him that will be news to Him. But He likes us so much that He's glad whenever we spend time with Him, and He never gets enough of our chatter. He never gets bored with us and our agenda.

Like all good listeners, He does a lot more listening than talking, but when He finally does speak He always has something worthwhile to say. And is it possible that He would be glad to talk more often if we'd just be quiet and give Him a chance to get a word in edgewise?

God's response is the most exciting part of prayer—and the most important. Since the primary purpose of prayer is communication, not information, and since we can't inform God of anything He doesn't already know, then His response is the more important part of the communication!

God wants to talk to us!

The Bible premise is that God *wants* to talk to us! Let's notice a few references on that. Jesus said to His disciples:

> Henceforth I call you not servants; for the servant knoweth not what his lord doeth: but I have called you friends (John 15:15).

One of the most significant aspects of friendship is that friends talk. They share. They communicate. There may not be much communication in the master/servant relationship or the employer/employee relationship. That may be limited to, "Take a letter, Miss Jones." But friends want to know what is going on in each other's lives because they care. What is important to us is also important to them—just *because* it's important to us. That's what makes friends. And that's what God is interested in sharing with us. He wants us to know what's going on. He wants us to be involved in *His* life.

On another occasion Jesus said, "I will love him, and will manifest myself to him" (John 14:21). He wants to manifest Himself to His friends. Those who are strangers or enemies are not given the same privilege of communication as are His friends. God is constantly seeking to *make* friends of everyone, including the strangers and enemies, but until they accept His friendship, He is unable to open to them His counsels. The closest communication with Him is reserved for those in His inner circle.

Let's look at one more reference. Jesus is speaking:

> Verily, verily, I say unto you, He that entereth not by the door into the sheepfold, but climbeth up some other way, the same is a thief and a robber. But he that entereth in by the door is the shepherd of the sheep. To him the porter openeth; and the sheep hear his voice; and he calleth his own sheep by name, and leadeth them out. And . . . he goeth before them, and the sheep follow him: for they know his voice. And a stranger will they not follow, but will flee from him: for they know not the voice of strangers (John 10:1-5).

Isn't it good to know that the Good Shepherd has a voice that His sheep can recognize, so that they won't be led astray by the voice of a stranger? How do we learn to recognize His voice? The answer is simple: By getting to know Him, through the day-by-day relationship with Him. That's all it takes.

If we come to Him in faith, He will speak His mysteries to us personally. Our hearts will often burn within us as One draws nigh to commune with us as He did with Enoch (*The Desire of Ages*, p. 668).

Prayer brings a response from God. His response may be Yes, and it may be No. There may be a delay in His response as He teaches us to wait upon Him, but to every sincere prayer will come a response. And when the answer is No, which is the exception to the rule insofar as the examples given in the Bible are concerned, God adds an explanation of why so that communication can continue.

He didn't leave Moses to wonder why he wasn't allowed into the Promised Land. He didn't leave David to wonder why he wasn't allowed to build the temple. He told them why He was saying No to their requests.

How God speaks

God's first preference for communication is face to face! He isn't happy with long-distance relationships. After the creation of mankind, He didn't stay in the heavenly throne room and send out memos. He came Himself, on a daily basis, to spend time walking in the Garden. He must have looked forward to that appointment all day long!

But when sin entered, God's plan was interrupted. No longer could He speak to us face to face. It would destroy us. So He began to use alternate methods for communication. He sent the angels (see Genesis 19:1; 2 Kings 1:3; Daniel 8:16; Luke 1:11). He spoke through visions and dreams (see Genesis 15:1; 1 Samuel 3:15; Daniel 2:19; Matthew 1:20). At times He spoke with an audible voice (see Exodus 20:1-17; Matthew 3:17). He used signs and symbols (see Exodus 4:8; Jeremiah 44:29; Luke 2:12). He sent His Son (see John 3:16; Mark 1:11). He sent the Holy Spirit (see John 14:16; Acts 2:2-4). At times God has spoken through earthquakes, fires, judgments, affliction, and trials. He has given us messages through the prophets and through the living preacher. He often speaks through the still, small voice. He speaks to us through His Word. He speaks to us through nature. He speaks to us through providential workings. He has invested all the creativity of a God of love to find ways to reach us with His messages of love and counsel.

As the basis for knowing when it is His voice that is speaking to us through the various methods He may use, He has given us His Word. His Word is to be the test. For although God speaks in many ways, His messages do not contradict each other. He will not command in one voice that which He has forbidden in another. God's voice is always in harmony with itself.

Since His Word has been established, any time we are in doubt as to whether a message is from Him, we can compare it to what has been revealed in His Word. But in order to understand His Word aright, we must have the help of the Holy Spirit, which is given in answer to prayer. Here we are back to the personal devotional life once again. If we want to communicate with God, and if we want to be sure when it is His voice speaking to our hearts, there is no substitute for our regular, private time with Him. It is difficult for God to get His messages through to us if we seek Him only when we're panicked or under stress. Communication with God is not intended to be used merely as a fire escape. But when we take time for regular, ongoing fellowship with Him, He can speak to us in times of crisis as well as in times of peace.

Two-way communication in prayer

Prayer was never intended to be a one-way street. If you will take the time, when you have finished with your part of the prayer, to allow God to speak to you, you may be surprised at what He has been waiting to reveal to you. Have you ever tried it? Here are some guidelines that some have found to be meaningful:

Be guided by His Word. Even the impressions that come to your mind during prayer must always be tested by His Word. This will prove a safeguard against error or fanaticism. If there appears to be disagreement between the messages you receive, *wait!* Wait for God to bring understanding and to make His voice plain and clear, so that you can know what He is trying to tell you.

Get away by yourself. If you want to hear God's voice clearly, find a quiet place, away from the interference of human voices. Sometimes the din is so heavy that it is difficult to hear clearly when the still, small voice is trying to speak.

When every other voice is hushed, and in quietness we wait before Him, the silence of the soul makes more distinct the voice of God (*The Desire of Ages*, p. 363).

Slow down. We are in too big of a hurry. We make our speeches to God and then run on our way, when we should allow time for Him to speak to our hearts.

Many, even in their seasons of devotion, fail of receiving the blessing of real communion with God. They are in too great haste. With hurried steps they press through the circle of Christ's loving presence, pausing perhaps a moment within the sacred precincts, but not waiting for counsel. They have no time to remain with the divine Teacher. With their burdens they return to their work. They must give themselves time to think, to pray, to wait upon God (*Education*, p. 260).

Watch for the peace. We can plan on peace—one of the fruits of the Spirit—in response to our prayers. One of the greatest indications that we have heard the voice of the Good Shepherd and not the voice of a stranger is the peace that comes with it. Have you experienced it? The devil may try to get mixed up in your prayers and force his own message into your mind, but he cannot bring peace. He may produce excitement or nice vibes or powerful feelings, but he cannot produce peace. The peace of the Spirit is one of the earmarks, or evidences, that it is God's voice you heard, not Satan's.

It keeps getting better and better. Only God can continually outdo Himself. Notice this paragraph from *The Desire of Ages*:

As men set forth the best wine first, then afterward that which is worse, so does the world with its gifts. That which it offers may please the eye and fascinate the senses, but it proves to be unsatisfying. The wine turns to bitterness, the gaiety to gloom. That which was begun with songs and mirth ends in weariness and disgust. But the gifts of Jesus are ever fresh and new. The feast that He provides for the soul never fails to give satisfaction and joy. Each new gift increases the capacity of the receiver to appreciate and enjoy the blessings of the Lord. He gives grace for grace. There can be no failure of supply. If you abide in Him, the fact that you receive a rich gift today insures the reception of a richer gift tomorrow. The words of Jesus to Nathanael express the law of God's dealing with the children of faith. With every fresh revelation of His love, He declares to the receptive heart, "Believest thou? thou shalt see greater things than these" (*The Desire of Ages*, p. 148).

He matches His words with ours. It happens too often to miss! God is in the habit of answering the questions that we ask Him. You may be praying about a particular thing, and often within just a day or two you will come across a verse or paragraph that speaks to that very question. Sometimes you may wonder how God does it! His Word adapts itself to every human dilemma. When you seek counsel from Him, He knows how to lead you to exactly the answer you need to hear.

Often He does this within the framework of your regular devotional life. At other times, He adds more creative means. Not long ago I heard about a woman who was facing a major decision in her life. She had been praying about what to do, and she wanted to be sure to do the right thing. She had a few days of vacation available, so she took her ten-year-old daughter with her to Yosemite National Park. She packed several devotional books, along with her Bible, and spent quite a bit of time reading, praying, and trying to decide what God wanted her to do.

One particular Bible text began to surface. She found it when she opened her Bible at random, trying to decide where she wanted to read. She found it again in a chapter she chose from *Patriarchs and Prophets*. The next afternoon she got out

The Desire of Ages, and guess what text she ran across. She began to suspect that God was trying to tell her something with that particular verse.

At the end of her third day she decided that she needed to take a break from the heavy reading, so she went to the store for some supplies. Along with the groceries she picked up a news magazine, and when she got back to camp she started thumbing through it. An article about a man who had been kidnapped caught her eye. He shared his story, and concluded by saying, "If there is one thing I have learned from this experience . . ."—and he quoted "her" text!

She threw down the magazine and started laughing and crying all at the same time. "OK, OK God, I get the message!" she exclaimed.

God is fully capable of getting His message across, so long as we continue to seek Him and wait for His answer to our prayers. He will sometimes surprise us with the unexpected methods He uses to make sure we understand what He is trying to tell us.

Here's another story about a verse of Scripture that was given to someone during a time of special need. This young mother believes that God led her to a particular verse on a particular morning. She was in a crisis, and the words spoke encouragement and comfort, but she had a hard time feeling that way. "I know you sent me this verse, Father," she prayed. "Thank You for it. But it's so cold. It would be so nice if you could send me a message like this with my name on it. It would be so nice if it said, Dear Mary." She thought what it must have meant to Cyrus, at the time of Daniel, to find his own name in the Bible!

But the thought passed, and her day began. That afternoon, her little girl came home from kindergarten. She brought with her a handmade card with a verse of Scripture printed on it. She had colored it carefully, and at the top she had written, "Dear Mary." She never called her mother by her first name, but that's what she wrote on the card that day—not dear *Mommy*, but "Dear Mary." You can be sure that card was stuck on the refrigerator door for a very long time! God had matched His answer to her request! She had no doubt that the message was from Him.

Patriarchs and Prophets says it this way: "He speaks to us in our own language, that we may better understand Him" (p. 106).

Father Abraham

As we try to put shoes on some of these principles for hearing and recognizing the voice of God when He speaks to us, let's take a look at a story from the life of Abraham. Abraham was a friend of God (see James 2:23). One night he was given an interesting revelation that sent him into real turmoil. He was told to take Isaac, his son—the son of the promise—and offer him as a sacrifice. I like the way *Patriarchs and Prophets* describes the experience:

> The command was expressed in words that must have wrung with anguish that father's heart: "Take now thy son, thine only son Isaac, whom thou lovest, . . . and offer him there for a burnt offering." Isaac was the light of his home, the solace of his old age, and above all else the inheritor of the promised blessing. The loss of such a son by accident or disease would have been heart rending to the fond father; it would have bowed down his whitened head with grief; but he was commanded to shed the blood of that son with his own hand. It seemed to him a fearful impossibility (page 148).

Was this the voice of God? Could God possibly ask such a thing? We would be quick to say, "Oh no, Abraham, you must be mistaken. Haven't you heard about the Ten Commandments? God said, 'Thou shalt not kill.' This must be the voice of a stranger."

Of one thing you may be sure: That thought didn't escape Abraham, because someone was only too happy to remind him of it!

> Satan was at hand to suggest that he must be

deceived, for the divine law commands, "Thou shalt not kill," and God would not require what He had once forbidden. Going outside his tent, Abraham looked up to the calm brightness of the unclouded heavens, and recalled the promise made nearly fifty years before, that his seed should be as innumerable as the stars. If this promise was to be fulfilled through Isaac, how could he be put to death? Abraham was tempted to believe that he might be under a delusion (*ibid.*).

Notice on what basis Satan questioned whether this could be the voice of God: The message did not seem to agree with what God had already told him. First was the command, "Thou shalt not kill." Second, God had said that Isaac was the son of the promise. "In his doubt and anguish he [Abraham] bowed upon the earth, and prayed, as he had never prayed before" (*ibid.*). Well, I guess so! You would too, wouldn't you?

[He prayed] for some confirmation of the command if he must perform this terrible duty. He remembered the angels sent to reveal to him God's purpose to destroy Sodom, and who bore to him the promise of this same son Isaac, and he went to the place where he had several times met the heavenly messengers, hoping to meet them again, and receive some further direction (*ibid.*).

Meditate on that for a moment, and let your imagination work with the scene. Watch Abraham stumbling through the darkness alone, hurrying to the spot where the angels had come before, hoping they would come again and explain the mystery to him. But they didn't show up. Not this time. He waited for a time, straining his eyes to see their approach, listening intently for some sound. But nothing. All was dark and silent.

Darkness seemed to shut him in; but the command of God was sounding in his ears, "Take now thy son, thine only son Isaac, whom thou lovest." That command must be obeyed, and he dared not delay. Day was approaching, and he must be on his journey (*ibid.*).

Abraham started out on the journey as he had been commanded, but he kept praying. It seemed impossible that God, who had said, "Thou shalt not kill," now wanted him to kill his son. But the first day ended, and he hadn't killed him yet!

Abraham kept praying, and walking. Isaac was still alive at the end of the second day. The third day came, and he was alive on the third day as well. God gave Abraham three days to work through the problem. At the end of the third day he saw a cloud of promise hovering over the mountain where he was headed. With it came the assurance that God was still in control and could handle things, even though Abraham couldn't understand.

Those three days were painful for Abraham, but he learned a most beautiful lesson in the process, and his unique understanding of the atonement has been handed down to us today. The ram, caught in the nearby thicket to replace his son, pointed to the Lamb of God that was to come.

What are you praying for today? Your prayer will be answered as surely as was the prayer of Abraham. God may wait until the last minute, but the answer will be given. The promise is sure. God *will* respond to the prayers of His people. There is no such thing as an unanswered prayer.

To every sincere prayer an answer will come. It may not come just as you desire, or at the time you look for it; but it will come in the way and at the time that will best meet your need (*Gospel Workers*, p. 258).

Chapter 13
Prayer and Fasting

He came to the college cafeteria every Wednesday. Oh, he was there on other days too. After all, he was a student at the college and used the cafeteria regularly. But he came *especially* on Wednesday. He brought his Bible with him, and he stayed the entire two hours that the cafeteria was open for lunch. He spent the time "witnessing." That's what he would say if anyone asked him why he was there: "I come on Wednesday to witness."

He would go from table to table, visiting with the various students. He would sit down and stare, as if hypnotized, at the progression of the forks from plates to mouths, and he would say, "That food sure smells good!"

Then he would take a moment to inquire about the health of each person at the table. All the while, he never took his eyes off the food! "Spaghetti is my favorite meal," he would say, then pause, and then continue wistfully, "They *always* serve spaghetti on Wednesdays."

Before long someone was sure to ask, "So why aren't you eating?"

His golden opportunity had arrived. Instantly would come the reply: "I'm fasting."

"Then why are you here in the cafeteria?"

"I use the time that I would ordinarily be eating to come and witness."

"How long have you been fasting?"

"Since dinner yesterday."

"You mean you haven't had anything to eat since this time yesterday?"

"That's right."

"Don't you get hungry?"

"Yes, but it's worth it. You know, our Lord fasted for forty days. I'd like to do that sometime. So far I've fasted for as long as three days at a time."

"I could never do that. I'd get too hungry!"

And so the conversation would go, until the interest of those at the table turned to other matters. Then he would excuse himself and go to a different table: "That food sure smells good!"

He was a new Christian, just in from the asphalt jungle. Perhaps he hadn't had time yet to read the words of Jesus:

> When ye fast, be not, as the hypocrites, of a sad countenance: for they disfigure their faces, that they may appear unto men to fast. Verily I say unto you, They have their reward. But thou, when thou fastest, anoint thine head, and wash thy face; that thou appear not unto men to fast, but unto thy Father which is in secret: and thy Father, which seeth in secret, shall reward thee openly (Matthew 6:16-18).

The most devout of the Pharisees at the time of Christ fasted twice each week. Fasting was popular in those days, perhaps more so than in today's society. Today we diet! And today we go jogging! The same principles might apply, don't you suppose? Or would that be taking it too far?

Jesus warned against doing any of our good works to be seen of men (see Matthew 23:5).

But the Bible often talks about fasting, usually in connection with special prayer. Esther and her friends fasted for three days before approaching the king with the problem of Haman (see Esther 4:15, 16). Jehoshaphat proclaimed a fast when the enemy approached (see 2 Chronicles 20:1-3). Daniel fasted for three weeks when he was seeking special help to understand the vision he had been given (see Daniel 10:1-3).

Moses, Elijah, and Jesus each fasted for forty days—and Moses did it twice! However, the insight from *Patriarchs and Prophets* indicates that for Moses at least, there was a supernatural sustaining from heaven that lifted him above the necessities of normal life. So this fast was different from that of Jesus, who experienced the weakness and hunger that normally accompany going without food.

It might be well to remind ourselves right from the start that Jesus' fast during His forty days in the wilderness was intended to be unique to Him. We are not called upon to follow His example. His fast was as our *Substitute* (see *Counsels on Diet and Foods*, p. 189).

Wrong reasons to fast

Since we began this subject on a somewhat negative note, let's continue in that vein long enough to notice three *wrong* reasons for fasting.

Fasting is not for the purpose of showing off. We already read the text on this from the Sermon on the Mount. The problem with the fasting practiced by the Pharisees was that they did it to be seen. Fasting was never intended to be used as a means of drawing attention to self.

Fasting is not an act of merit. There is no merit in fasting. We do not earn God's favor or mercy by fasting. The Jews had lost sight of God's free grace, and, therefore, had come to believe that fasting would somehow recommend them to God. "Fasting was practiced by the Jews as an act of merit" (*The Desire of Ages*, p. 276).

Fasting is not intended to impress God. Fasting is not some sort of heavenly hunger strike by which we force God into a corner by refusing to eat. There is nothing we can do to make God willing to answer our prayers. He is *already* willing. He doesn't need our fasting or our penance or our sleeping on some bed of spikes. Whatever value there is in fasting is for us, not for Him. We are the ones who will be changed. Our fastings and our prayers are not for the purpose of changing God.

Right reasons to fast

However, fasting is legitimate when it is done in the right way and for the right reason:

> There are times before us that will try the souls of men, and there will be need of watchfulness, of *the right kind of fasting* (Ellen G. White Comments, *SDA Bible Commentary*, vol. 5, p. 1086).

Fasting may promote better physical health. This is a down-to-earth reason for fasting. In some physical conditions fasting promotes healing. If you need to fast for health reasons, that's certainly legitimate. If you'd like to study this more, read *The Ministry of Healing*, page 235.

Fasting can give a clear mind. Fasting may give you such a headache that you can't think at all! However, there are times when you will be able to think more clearly if you abstain from food. For those of us who get the headaches, there is more than one method for fasting, as we will notice in a few minutes. When Jesus went into the wilderness to fast, His purpose was to spend time considering His mission and communing with His Father as He prepared to take up the duties of public ministry. Daniel fasted for three weeks in order to understand the vision he had been given. Speaking of the early days of the Advent message, Ellen White makes this comment: "Often we fasted, that we might be better fitted to understand the truth" (*Counsels on Diet and Foods*, p. 187).

Fasting is acceptable when you can't help but fast. Perhaps you have experienced this kind of fasting. There are times when it is easier to fast than it is *not* to fast. Have you ever been faced with a great crisis, when the pressure was so intense that you just didn't feel like eating? Maybe you even forgot to eat! This kind of fasting isn't something you plan to do. It isn't something that you do because someone recommended it to you. It happens spontaneously, because of your great need. So there are right reasons for fasting, as well as wrong reasons. Fasting and prayer for the right reasons can be a real blessing. Fasting and prayer for the wrong reasons is worthless.

What is fasting?

This may seem rather elementary, but let's take just a few paragraphs to consider the various methods of fasting. There are more kinds of fasting than total abstinence. Some of us who are prone to the headaches are glad of this fact! Daniel 10 gives one example. Daniel didn't go without food for three weeks. He "ate no pleasant bread, neither . . . flesh nor wine" (Daniel 10:3). Ellen White suggests:

> They [the people of God] should set aside days for fasting and prayer. Entire abstinence from food may not be required, but they should eat sparingly of the most simple food (*Counsels on Diet and Foods*, pp. 188, 189).

Another insight given on the same pages is that *short* fasts can be beneficial—a day or two, or even a meal or two. God is reasonable. He who created our bodies knows about our need for food and water. The major premise for fasting is that it is always to be the exception, rather than the rule. Fasting is for times of special need. It is not intended to be a way of life. In the examples given in Scripture, the major fasts were primarily a once-in-a-lifetime experience. They weren't a regular part of life.

It is interesting to notice that fasting can include issues other than food and drink:

> The Word of God is not half comprehended. If each one would proclaim a fast for his own soul, studying the Word of God with earnest prayer, and reading only those books which would help him to gain a clearer knowledge of the Word, God's people would have much more spiritual health and strength, much more spiritual knowledge and understanding, than they now reveal. We need to seek God, that we may find Him precious to our

souls. We need to keep Him as our abiding guest and companion, never parting from Him (*This Day With God*, p. 150).

This kind goeth not out but by prayer and fasting

This brings us to the foot of the Mount of Transfiguration, with the nine disciples who were waiting for Jesus to return. You remember the story. The disciples had been given power over unclean spirits and rejoiced that even the devils were subject unto them (see Luke 10:17). When this father brought his son, asking that he be healed, the disciples were ready to do the job! No one was more surprised than they at their lack of success.

They were relieved, as well as embarrassed, when Jesus returned from His night on the mountain and took care of the problem. But they didn't understand. After the crowds had gone away, they asked Him, "Why weren't we able to cast this one out?"

Jesus replied, "This kind goes out only by prayer and fasting" (see Mark 9:29).

People have often concluded, on the basis of this story, that there are two kinds of devils: the easy kind and the hard kind. For the easy kind, you can just tell them to leave; but for the hard kind, you have to spend some time in prayer and fasting first, or they won't obey you.

But this doesn't make sense. In the first place, if that were true, Jesus should have told the disciples to spend the day in prayer and fasting and ask the father to come again the next day. After all, how were they to know they were going to be asked to cast out a demon that day? They couldn't fast *all* the time, just in case one of the bad kind showed up, could they?

In the second place, so far as we know, Jesus Himself hadn't been fasting. Since it was early in the morning he probably hadn't had breakfast yet, but there is nothing to indicate that He had been fasting prior to that.

So what was Jesus talking about?

Fasting is an attitude more than a ritual. The one who is fasting for the right reasons is saying, My dependence upon

God is more vital to me than even food and drink. The disciples were unable to cast out this demon—or any other demon—so long as they were depending upon their own strength. Jesus wasn't talking about "the bad kind" when He said, "this kind goes out only by prayer and fasting." *Any* kind goes out only by prayer and fasting! The weakest of the forces of evil are stronger than we are. The strongest can be overcome in the strength of Jesus.

The disciples had lost sight of Jesus. They had spent the night grumbling because they were left behind at the foot of the mountain, and feeling jealous at the thought of what they might be missing. There wasn't a demon in all of Satan's hosts that they could have overpowered in that condition!

Which brings us once again to the day-by-day relationship with God. It is through fellowship with Him, through prayer and the study of His Word, that we come to depend upon His power instead of upon our own.

One of the most common excuses that is given for not spending time alone with God day by day is, "I don't have time." But do you have time to eat? If you have time to eat each day, then you have time to spend with God each day! The problem is not a lack of time—it is a matter of priorities. When we say we don't have time, what we really mean is, "It isn't that important to me."

For Jesus, nothing was more important than His communion with His Father. He gained strength through the time He spent alone with God, just as we must do. He had no advantage over us in depending upon God's power rather than His own. If His disciples had spent time in prayer and communion with God during that night at the foot of the mountain, they would have been ready to heal the demon-possessed boy.

To have an attitude of fasting means that your private time with God is so important to you, and so high on your list of priorities, that if you ever are so pressed for time that you have to make a choice between physical food and spiritual food, you will always choose the spiritual food. *That* is true fasting!

Chapter 14
Thy Will Be Done

Recently a group got together to pray for a little boy who had a terminal disease. They said, "Of course God doesn't want this little boy to die! We don't believe in a God who wants children to die. It would be an insult to God, a lack of faith, to say 'Thy will be done' in such a case."

So they prayed. Afterward one of their group reported, "And we didn't pray any of that 'Thy will be done' stuff!"

Do you agree with that? Does it show a lack of faith or a misunderstanding of the character of God to pray, "Thy will be done"? Or is it safe to pray according to His will? We have been given some specific counsel on this point:

It is not always safe to ask for unconditional healing. Let your prayer include this thought: "Lord, Thou knowest every secret of the soul. Thou art acquainted with these persons; for Jesus, their advocate, gave His life for them. He loves them better than we possibly can. If, therefore . . ."

I remember praying with a group at the bedside of a dying man, and when someone said, "If it be Thy will," someone else in the group said, "Don't say *if!* That shows a lack of faith!" But notice the counsel we have been given:

"If, therefore, it is for Thy glory and the good of these afflicted ones to raise them up in health, we ask Thee in the name of Jesus, that health may be given them at this time." In a petition of this kind, no lack of faith is manifested. ... We should say after our earnest petition: "Nevertheless not my will, but Thine, be done." ... Such a petition will never be registered in heaven as a faithless prayer (*Counsels on Health*, p. 375).

So we are safe to pray for God's will to be done—and, in fact, it is unsafe *not* to pray according to His will. Now it is true, there are some things about which His will has already been revealed. We do not need to say, "And please forgive our sins, if it be Thy will," because His will has already been revealed on that one. It is *always* His will to forgive sin. But when it comes to requests for temporal blessings, we are to commit our requests to Him, and ask Him to work according to what He sees is best.

Limits to God's power

God is limited in what He can accomplish for us. Do you believe that? It's true. He's limited in a number of ways. It is true that we believe that God has all power in heaven and in earth. But because of His involvement in the great controversy, His power still has limits. There are two ways in which God's power is limited.

God is limited by our power of choice. God decided right to begin with that all of His children would have the power of choice. He wasn't interested in having a bunch of robots in His kingdom, offering tape-recorded praise. He wanted only the service of love—and love has to be voluntary in order to be real.

God has done everything possible to win us to Himself. The cross opens its friendly arms to everyone born into this world. The invitation has been given to all. But God cannot force anyone to accept it. It would be contrary to His nature. Therefore, He is limited by our power of choice.

So when you read the Bible promise, "I will contend with him that contendeth with thee, and I will save thy children" (Isaiah 49:25), that's a conditional promise. God is limited there. He will do everything a God of love can do to bring your children to the point of accepting His love, but He will never force their will. Their power of choice always remains sacred.

God is limited by the bigger issues. There are times when God's hands are tied because of bigger issues at stake than the crisis of the moment. Jesus experienced it in Gethsemane. He would just as soon have skipped Gethsemane and the cross. It was not pleasant for Him. He felt the pain of a breaking heart as deeply as we do. When they came for Him there in the garden, tied His hands, and led Him away, He had to go, because there was bigger business than just *His* personal comfort.

Peter swung his sword and cut off an ear. Jesus said to His captors, "Just let me do this much"—and He reached out and healed the high priest's servant. But then He submitted to all that they could do, because He had a world that needed salvation. And He knew that in order to accomplish that, He could not escape the suffering.

So we don't have to look over our glasses at God and wonder if He's the sort of Being who likes to see little children die. When He has to say No to some of our requests today, it's because there is more at stake than just the momentary suffering of this life. His first priority is ending the great controversy so that the root of the problem, the world of sin, will be forever taken care of.

To use a rather homey illustration, I had my appendix out on my thirteenth birthday! It wasn't much fun, as birthday presents go! But after I got home and had a few more days to heal, my father was given the privilege of taking out the suture.

Instead of a series of single stitches, they had used one long stitch that went around and around, across the incision, with one end of the thread on one side and the other end on the other side. In order to remove the stitch, that thread had to be pulled all the way through.

My father took a pair of pliers and went to work. It hurt! Probably it hurt my father even more than it hurt me—and that was quite a bit! My father would just as soon have skipped that part. But he knew that there would be greater pain down the road somewhere if he didn't keep at it. So he gritted his teeth and finished the job.

When my boy was a teenager, he had a Honda motorcycle that wouldn't start. We were towing it behind the car, and he made the mistake of tying the rope to the handlebars instead of just holding on to it. He did a two and a half gainer and landed on the gravel, with gravel ground into his arm and shoulder.

I took him to the doctor. Now that was a mean thing to do! The doctor took a steel brush and some kind of cleansing solution, and scraped out the gravel that had been imbedded in the flesh. It was terribly painful. Why did we do it? Why were we so mean? Because we wanted to avoid greater pain further down the line.

Apparently, in some of our experiences in this life, God has to allow the pain and the disappointment and the tears, because He sees things that we can't see in terms of the bigger picture. He is committed to making sure that sin doesn't rise up a second time. For this reason, God's *preference* has to bow to His *wisdom*. His heart often has to give in to His better judgment, and He has to say No at times when He desperately longs to say Yes.

So we are safe in committing ourselves to His will. Because of His infinite love, just as often as He possibly can, He will give us the things for which we ask. He will spare us just as much suffering as possible. But because of His great wisdom, He will also refuse our requests when it would interfere with our greater good. We can come to Him with confidence and pray, "Thy will be done."

Chapter 15
Pray and Work

It is impossible to have a meaningful prayer life very long without becoming involved in service, and it is impossible to be involved in meaningful service very long without becoming involved in prayer. The two are inseparable.

Many have had the stereotype of witness as going down the street ringing doorbells, and talking religion to people they've never seen before. But work in the Christian life—service and witness and outreach—can involve any number of methods. The important thing is to work. One of the greatest reasons why prayer life has become little more than a form for many people is that they have not become involved in service and work for others.

Notice the story of the feeding of the 5,000:

When Jesus then lifted up his eyes, and saw a great company come unto him, he saith unto Philip, Whence shall we buy bread, that these may eat? And this he said to prove him: for he himself knew what he would do. Philip answered him, Two hundred pennyworth of bread is not sufficient for them, that every one of them may take a little. One of his disciples, Andrew, Simon Peter's brother, saith unto him, There is a lad here, which hath five barley loaves, and two small fishes: but what are they among so many? And Jesus said, Make the men sit down. Now there was much grass in the place. So the men sat down, in number about five thousand. And

Jesus took the loaves; and when he had given thanks, he distributed to the disciples, and the disciples to them that were set down; and likewise of the fishes as much as they would. When they were filled, he said unto his disciples, Gather up the fragments that remain, that nothing be lost. Therefore they gathered them together, and filled twelve baskets with the fragments of the five barley loaves; which remained over and above unto them that had eaten (John 6:5-13).

Let's read Mark's account to get his insights on the relationship of prayer to Christian service:

> When the day was now far spent, his disciples came unto him, and said, This is a desert place, and now the time is far passed: Send them away, that they may go into the country round about, and into the villages, and buy themselves bread: for they have nothing to eat. He answered and said unto them, Give ye them to eat. And they say unto him, Shall we go and buy two hundred pennyworth of bread, and give them to eat? He saith unto them, How many loaves have ye? go and see. And when they knew, they say, Five and two fishes. And he commanded them to make all sit down by companies upon the green grass. And they sat down in ranks, by hundreds, and by fifties. And when he had taken the five loaves and the two fishes, he looked up to heaven, and blessed, and brake the loaves, and gave them to his disciples to set before them; and the two fishes divided he among them all. And they did all eat, and were filled (Mark 6:35-42).

Jesus "looked up to heaven." (As far as we can tell, Jesus prayed with His eyes open that day! I wish I had known that when I was a boy! The guilt I used to have if I peeked during prayer was terrible. We have our own traditions, don't we? We probably have just as many traditions as the people in Christ's day, and this is one of them.) But Jesus wasn't operating independently here. He accomplished all of His miracles through prayer, through the power from above Him rather than through the power from within Him. His life of prayer and service for others is an example for us today.

How would you like to have been one of the disciples that day? If there were 5,000 men, and they had 5,000 wives, and brought their 10,000 children, how many people were there altogether? Get out your pocket calculator and figure it out!

Then there were twelve disciples. Each disciple had to take food to how many people? More than 1,500 each! How would you like to be told that 1,500 people were coming for dinner—and dinner would be served immediately! Can you see the disciples starting out into the crowd, carrying the little baskets of bread and fish? Do you think they were afraid of making fools of themselves? It sounds pretty exciting to read about it, but it must have been stressful for the disciples, because the next time they had a chance to do the same thing, when the 4,000 were in need of food, they weren't that eager to try it again. In fact, they were reluctant and tried to talk Jesus out of it!

For the multitude it was more exciting. They may have been a little slower than the disciples to understand the extent of the problem before them. They were hungry, but they hadn't been expecting supper! They weren't put on the spot like the disciples were, so they were able to sit back and enjoy the miracle far more. Can you imagine yourself in the crowd? Can you imagine watching the progress of the disciples, wondering if there would still be some left by the time it came your turn? Perhaps you have experienced something like that at a potluck dinner! But sure enough—there was bread for everyone. No one was left out. Not only did everyone have plenty to eat, but there were as many baskets left over as there were disciples.

And the moral of the story is . . .

Not only was this a miracle which provided for the needs of the hungry crowd there in Galilee; it was also an acted parable. There are at least seven principles regarding prayer and work that we can learn from this story.

We cannot give to others that which we do not ourselves possess. That's a quote, by the way! It's found in *Mount of Blessing*, page 37: "We cannot give to others that which we do not ourselves possess." One of the problems many of us have had in trying to be witnesses for Christ is that we have experienced nothing about which to witness! If we have not tasted and seen that the Lord is good, we will have real trouble describing the experience to someone else. If you've never tasted strawberry shortcake, or even seen strawberry shortcake, you'll have a hard time sharing with someone else what strawberry shortcake is like. We cannot give to others what we ourselves do not possess.

We are required to give to others what we ourselves do not possess. Now are your brains twisted all out of shape? At first glance, these first two points seem to be fighting each other, don't they? You can't give to someone else what you don't have yourself—but you have to! Oddly, that's the way it is! The disciples, the day the 5,000 were fed, did not have bread enough to feed the crowd. In fact, the disciples themselves didn't have any bread at all—the little boy had to help them out, even to get started! Then Jesus said to them, "Give ye them to eat." What an impossible command! They couldn't give bread to the multitude if they had no bread themselves—yet that is exactly what they were required to do.

The disciples must have had a degree of faith in order to become involved in service that day on the mountainside. But as they worked in union with the One who lifted up His eyes to heaven, somehow the miracle happened. That's always the source of supply for the needs of those around us. We have to receive it first, in order to give it. And then, as we rely upon the One who has the abundance, we can give to others what we ourselves don't possess.

We can impart only that which we receive from Christ; and we can receive only as we impart to others. That quote is from *The Desire of Ages,* page 370. As we continue imparting, we continue receiving; and the more we impart, the more we will receive. We can't give away more than we receive, nor can we receive any more than we give. The more the disciples gave, the more they had to give. That's always God's method of working. Even when it comes to tithes and offerings—we get more by giving away what we have. It's a principle that the world doesn't understand, but it is one of the greatest principles of God's kingdom.

Do you want to become involved in outreach and service? Reach out with what you have in your hand right now, and when you do, you will receive more. If you hoard what you have right now, you'll lose it.

He who does nothing but pray will soon cease to pray. Ellen White once said:

> God does not mean that any of us should become hermits or monks and retire from the world in order to devote ourselves to acts of worship. The life must be like Christ's life—between the mountain and the multitude. He who does nothing but pray will soon cease to pray, or his prayers will become a formal routine. When men take themselves out of social life, away from the sphere of Christian duty and cross bearing; when they cease to work earnestly for the Master, who worked earnestly for them, they lose the subject matter of prayer and have no incentive to devotion. Their prayers become personal and selfish. They cannot pray in regard to the wants of humanity or the upbuilding of Christ's kingdom, pleading for strength wherewith to work (*Steps to Christ*, p. 101).

Prayer is essential. Prayer is the starting place. Christ didn't send His disciples out with the five loaves and two fish, and *then* start praying. He took time to pray to begin with. But He didn't stop there. He didn't pray and then wait for manna to be rained from heaven into the laps of the people. Prayer and work always go together. Prayer alone is not enough.

If the work is of God, He will provide the means. It is not our problem to provide the resources sufficient for accomplishing God's work. This never has been our problem, and it never *will* be our problem. That is God's department.

The means in our possession may not seem to be sufficient for the work; but if we will move forward in faith, believing in the all-sufficient power of God, abundant resources will open before us. If the work be of God, He Himself will provide the means for its accomplishment. He will reward honest, simple reliance upon Him. The little that is wisely and economically used in the service of the Lord of heaven will increase in the very act of imparting. In the hand of Christ the small supply of food remained undiminished until the famished multitude were satisfied. If we go to the Source of all strength, with our hands of faith outstretched to receive, we shall be sustained in our work, even under the most forbidding circumstances, and shall be enabled to give to others the bread of life (*The Desire of Ages*, p. 371).

This is not talking simply about bread. In fact, when Jesus fed the multitude, He was not offering them just bread. They missed the point and came around looking for some more free meals—and Jesus rebuked them. He said, You're just here because of the loaves and fishes.

The promise of this acted parable is that whatever resources are needed for carrying out the work of God, whether temporal, physical, or spiritual, all will be provided through the same method. If the work is His work, He will provide the means for its accomplishment, no matter what means are needed.

We are invited to bring our barley loaves to Jesus. When Andrew started looking around through the crowd to see how much food was on hand, the little lad he found didn't look too impressive. He didn't have much. But when he brought what he had to Jesus, all of a sudden it was enough and to spare.

In today's world there is an expert in every field you can imagine. The correct procedure for big business operations is that you call in the experts. When we've got problems, it's considered a wise investment to pay all travel and other expenses to get the professionals into town.

God's kingdom works on the same principle! We are invited to call in the Expert! But we sometimes get mixed up about who the Expert really is. Listen to these words:

> When the question comes home to your heart, "Whence shall we buy bread, that these may eat?" let not your answer be the response of unbelief. When the disciples heard the Saviour's direction, "Give ye them to eat," all the difficulties arose in their minds. They questioned, Shall we go away into the villages to buy food? So now, when the people are destitute of the bread of life, the Lord's children question, Shall we send for someone from afar, to come and feed them? But what said Christ? "Make the men sit down," and He fed them there. . . . Commune with Him. Bring your barley loaves to Jesus (*ibid.*, pp. 370, 371).

The disciples thought the villages were the source of bread—when the Bread of life was standing right beside them! We sometimes think that others in the church have the wisdom needed. But we don't have to get it from others—we can go to the Source of wisdom, and He will supply our need just as willingly as He will supply theirs.

When you see the needs of those around you, don't try to delegate the responsibility. *You* are invited to the Source of all strength. Bring your barley loaves to Jesus. He is willing and waiting to bless.

Service and outreach drive us to prayer. Nothing will make you more aware of your desperate need for help from above than to become involved in reaching out to others.

> If you will go to work as Christ designs that His disciples shall, and win souls for Him, you will feel the need of a deeper experience and a greater knowledge in divine things, and will hunger and thirst after righteousness. You will plead with God, and your faith will be strengthened, and your soul will drink deeper drafts at

the well of salvation. Encountering opposition and trials will drive you to the Bible and prayer. You will grow in grace and the knowledge of Christ, and will develop a rich experience (*Steps to Christ*, p. 80).

Prayer goes stale without service. Bible study becomes blah without service. Your devotional life will become nothing but routine and ritual if you fail to become involved in sharing with others what you are receiving from God. You will stop receiving if you stop giving.

And the more you reach out, the more your prayer life will grow and flourish. Do you want a more meaningful prayer life? Find ways to give away what you have been receiving from Him, and you will be prepared to receive more abundantly of His gifts.

Chapter 16
Prayer and Praise

How would you feel if someone walked up to you and said, "Oh, thank you. Thank you so much. I just can't begin to thank you. You are so wonderful. You are so great. Thanks a million!" You might be somewhat embarrassed if someone were that enthusiastic—but wouldn't you want to ask, "Thanks for *what*?"

And what if they replied, "I don't know. But thank you so much!" You might wonder if they had gone jolly 'round the bend.

The most important principle for giving praise and thanksgiving to God is that there has to be *content*. There has to be something more to praise than just saying "Hallelujah" over and over. Praise and thanksgiving must be a response to specific blessings or evidences of His love, not just empty words.

Psalm 47:7 says, "Sing ye praises *with understanding*" (emphasis supplied). God is only interested in worship that comes from the heart. In his book *Disciple*, Pentecostal author Juan Carlos Ortiz writes:

> In order to teach my congregation about praise, I began to question them. When someone said, "Praise the Lord," I said, "Wait a minute. Why do you praise the Lord?"
>
> "Well, I praise the Lord because . . . uh, well, . . ." He didn't know.
>
> Someone else said "Hallelujah!" And I said, "Why did

175

you say Hallelujah?"

"Well, I said Hallelujah because, . . . uh, well . . ."

"You said Hallelujah because you're a Pentecostal! That's why you did. It's part of our way. That's why."

David said, "Praise Him for His mighty *deeds*." We haven't done that. We have come to church with wheelbarrows full of wrapped boxes tied with nice ribbons and big cards, reading "Allelujah," "Praise the Lord," "Glory to God," and "Amen." And the pastors have said," What wonderful people! They come to church with so much praise!" And all the boxes have been brought to the altar. But when God has opened all of His presents, He has found nothing inside."

Seventh-day Adventists don't even bring the boxes! We believe in being much more dignified about our religion. We may not say the words as often, but we may be just as unmindful of the blessings from God.

Regardless of your method for praising God, whether you find it easy to say, "Praise the Lord," or whether you thank Him privately, in order to be meaningful, praise and thanksgiving must have content. We are to make our praise specific—and aren't there plenty of specific blessings for which to praise God? Sure there are!

Basics of prayer

Praise is not to be a formal routine. Praise is an individual thing. My method may be entirely different from yours, and yours may be different from someone else's.

I still remember with pleasure the seminary student who attended a week of prayer that my brother and I conducted at Andrews University. This seminary student sat on the back row. He had a deep voice. He didn't say "Allelujah" or "Amen." He didn't just sit quietly listening. He said, "That's all *right!*" It was his way, and I liked it!

Here's a paragraph from *The Ministry of Healing*:

Our confession of His faithfulness is Heaven's chosen

agency for revealing Christ to the world. We are to acknowledge His grace as made known through holy men of
old; but that which will be most effectual is the testimony
of our own experience. We are witnesses for God as we
reveal in ourselves the working of a power that is divine.
Every individual has a life distinct from all others, and an
experience differing essentially from theirs. God desires
that our praise shall ascend to Him, marked with our own
individuality. These precious acknowledgements to the
praise of the glory of His grace, when supported by a
Christlike life, have an irresistible power that works for
the salvation of souls (*The Ministry of Healing*, p. 100).

Notice the emphasis upon the individuality of our praise.
Do you have your own unique method for praising God?
"That's all *right!*" Here are some other good ideas about
prayer and praise.

We don't praise God nearly enough. Israel experienced
God's deliverance time and time again. They received blessing
after blessing from Him, but they quickly forgot what He had
done for them. Instead of offering praise, they offered com-
plaints (see Psalms 105, 106).

We are told that if we praised God every time we had an
evidence of His love and care for us, we would be continually
praising Him. It's so easy instead to take His blessings for
granted, isn't it?

We are invited to praise in good times—and in bad times.
We don't have to wait to praise God until something good happens. We are invited to praise Him when things are going
wrong. "Praise the Lord even when you fall into darkness.
Praise Him even in temptation" (*Testimonies*, vol. 2, p. 593).

But why would you want to praise God when things go
wrong? What can you find to praise Him about then?

The story is told of an old preacher who was walking to
town one day and met a robber who took all that he had. That
evening he wrote in his diary, "Today I was robbed, and I
praise God for the following reasons: first, that I have never
been robbed before. Second, that although he took my money,

he did not take my life. Third, although he took all I had, it wasn't much! And fourth, I am thankful that it was I who was robbed, and not I who robbed."

Even in the darkest times of our lives, we can be thankful for the light that we have had before. We can be thankful for the light we are promised up ahead. And we can be thankful for the One who stays with us, even in the darkness. We may not be able to sense His presence, but we can *know* He's there.

Praise . . . is as much a duty as is prayer. You probably recognize that as a quote! It's from *Christ's Object Lessons*, page 299. Do you like the sound of praise that is offered as a *duty*? How about the prayer that is a duty? Sometimes we look at the word *duty* as a four-letter-word! But is *duty* a bad word? Ellen White adds this illumination to duty:

> When once the gaze is fixed upon [Christ], the life finds its center. . . . Duty becomes a delight and sacrifice a pleasure (*Education*, p. 297).

We don't approach duty with gritted teeth and clenched jaw. We put our attention toward beholding Christ and becoming acquainted with Him. Then we can rephrase it in our own experience: "Praise is as much a delight as is prayer."

How to praise God

There are a number of ways to praise God. If you are looking for as many ways as possible to make your experience of praise a delight, perhaps you will want to consider some of the methods used by others in their worship of God.

We can praise God in song. Paul and Silas used this method when they were in jail. Do you remember the result? God responded to their praise in a spectacular way.

One time I met two students at Pacific Union College who had been into black witchcraft. They had experienced the miracle of conversion. I asked them "Do the spirits ever come around now that you have been converted?"

They said, "Oh yes. We recognize them well."

"What do you do?"

"We sing songs of praise. When we sing songs of praise, the spirits don't like it. They have to leave. They cannot bear to listen."

There is power in praise. Perhaps this is why we have been told that singing is as much a part of worship as is prayer. The psalms were often set to music, and are filled with praise to God for what He has done for His people in the past.

> Let praise and thanksgiving be expressed in song. When tempted, instead of giving utterance to our feelings, let us by faith lift up a song of thanksgiving to God (*The Ministry of Healing*, p. 254).

We can praise God privately. Prayer doesn't have to be public in order to praise God. We can praise Him privately as well. If you wish to express appreciation to some friend of yours, you don't have to pay for a spot on the evening news or run an ad in the newspaper. You can speak to that person personally.

The same is true of our praise to God. At times we will *want* to share with others through a public statement of thanksgiving for His blessings to us. But perhaps the most personal worship and praise will be private.

> We do not pray any too much, but we are too sparing of giving thanks. We are the constant recipients of God's mercies, and yet how little gratitude we express, how little we praise Him for what He has done for us (*Steps to Christ*, p. 103).

We can praise God by witnessing to what He has done for us. Here is one of the reasons why Christians should witness. As we share with others what God has done for us, their interest is often aroused. They are drawn to Him as He is uplifted through our praise.

The demoniacs who wanted to follow Jesus were told to go back home and tell what great things God had done for *them*. This avenue for outreach is available to every Christian. You may not be skilled in presenting doctrinal arguments, but you can tell what He has done in your life, and often that testimony makes more of an impression than theological discussion ever could.

We can praise continually. Psalm 34:1 says, "I will bless the Lord at all times: his praise shall continually be in my mouth. And Psalm 35:28: "My tongue shall speak of thy righteousness and of thy praise all the day long." Praising is not to be confined to the church or the closet. Praise is to become a way of life. We have been told to "pray without ceasing"—we are also invited to praise without ceasing! "God desired that the whole life of His people should be a life of praise" (*Christ's Object Lessons*, p. 299).

Praise is a battle song! You can read about this in 2 Chronicles 20. The enemy was coming, so Jehoshaphat called the people together for a prayer meeting. They fasted and prayed, and God sent them His instructions: Go out to meet the enemy, led by a choir!

It was a singular way of going to battle against the enemy's army—praising the Lord with singing, and exalting the God of Israel. *This was their battle song.* They possessed the beauty of holiness. If more praising of God were engaged in now, hope and courage and faith would steadily increase. And would not this strengthen the hands of the valiant soldiers who today are standing in defense of truth? (*Prophets and Kings*, p. 202, emphasis supplied).

Our human tendency, when facing a crisis, is to fight for ourselves—or perhaps, when we see we cannot possibly overcome, to run to God and beg for His protection. He wants us to come to Him for deliverance, and we can come the way Jehoshaphat and his army came, with songs of praise instead of fearful and tearful pleas. He honors the faith that praises Him *before* the battle is won, not just afterward!

The benefits of praise

The benefits of praise are numerous. Praise is not just good for God—it's good for us! That's one of the beautiful aspects of God's kingdom. He always arranges to give back to us whatever we give to Him—and with interest! The more we praise Him for His blessings, the more we are blessed. Notice some of the specific ways, along with the inspired comments for reference.

More praise equals more power in prayer.

If the loving-kindness of God called forth more thanksgiving and praise, we would have far more power in prayer. We would abound more and more in the love of God and have more bestowed to praise Him for. You who complain that God does not hear your prayers, change your present order and mingle praise with your petitions. When you consider His goodness and mercies you will find that He will consider your wants (*Testimonies*, vol. 5, p. 317).

More praise equals more victory.

The exercise of praise "drives back the power of Satan." It expels the spirit of murmuring and complaint, and the tempter loses ground (*Christ's Object Lessons*, p. 300).

If there was much more praising the Lord, and far less doleful recitation of discouragements, many more victories would be achieved (*Evangelism*, p. 499).

More praise equals more faith.

If more praising of God were engaged in now, hope and courage and faith would steadily increase (*Prophets and Kings*, p. 202; see also *The Ministry of Healing*, p. 100).

More praise equals more efficiency in service.

Efficiency in His service would be greatly increased by recounting His goodness and His wonderful works in behalf of His children (*Christ's Object Lessons*, p. 300).

More praise equals more souls won to Christ.

No more effective means can be employed for winning souls to Christ (*ibid.*).

More praise equals more physical health.

Nothing tends more to promote health of body and of soul than does a spirit of gratitude and praise (*The Ministry of Healing*, p. 251).

More praise equals a closer relationship with God.

The soul may ascend nearer heaven on the wings of praise (*Steps to Christ*, p. 104).

More praise equals more glory for God.

Whoso offereth praise glorifieth me (Psalm 50:23).

So praise the Lord! Praise Him for who He is, for His love and mercy and kindness. Praise Him for what He has done in the past. Praise Him for what He is doing for you today. Praise Him for the promise of what He is going to do in the future. We can praise Him not only in words, but by consecrating to Him all that we are and have.

Would you like to offer to God the greatest praise possible? The greatest praise is to become consecrated channels through whom He can work (see *The Acts of the Apostles*, p. 566). You are invited to do that today!

Chapter 17
Why Things Get Worse When We Pray

When I first began to seek a personal relationship with Jesus, I had been a minister for three years and had come into great trouble. For three years I had relied on second-hand sermons. I had preached Richards and Fagal and Everson and my father and my uncle. But there was no power because I didn't know God for myself.

In my desperate study to find an answer to my problem, I was led to an understanding of the importance of Bible study and prayer for myself—for my own soul, not just for my job. I began to set aside time every day to seek Him and was dumbfounded to discover that everything went wrong. Not only did more trials and problems come to confront me, but I actually lived a worse life than I had before.

So I quit. I quit seeking Jesus for myself. To my surprise, everything went better! My initial reaction was, "That proves it! This business of seeking God doesn't work."

But within a couple of weeks I fell so hard that I changed my mind again. I said, "Looks like I need Jesus, after all." Again I began to seek Him day by day, and again everything caved in. And I quit again, because it wasn't working.

I'd hate to admit how long this cycle kept up. Some of us are slow to learn. We can send a message around the world at the speed of 186,000 miles per second, but we can't get the same message through one quarter inch of human skull!

I found it easy to figure out why the devil would work the way he had. It was easy to see why he would want to do everything possible to discourage me from seeking a relationship with God. But where was *God*? Wasn't He big enough to keep this kind of thing from happening? This was a mystery for a long time, until one day the Bible explained it clearly.

The story of Job

I am glad to tell you that I found the answer to this question when I read the book of Job. Let's begin reading in Job 1:6:

> Now there was a day when the sons of God came to present themselves before the Lord, and Satan came also among them.

What was *he* doing there? Well, Adam had sold out to Satan, so Satan now claimed this world as his kingdom. Satan was there in the counsel of heaven, representing this world.

> And the Lord said unto Satan, Whence comest thou?
> Then Satan answered the Lord, and said, From going to and fro in the earth, and from walking up and down in it (verse 7).

In other words, I'm in charge down there. The people are following me. We're paraphrasing now, you understand. God said, "You think you're in charge? Wait a minute! Have you considered my servant Job?"

What was Satan's response? He said, "Job? Ha! It looks like the reason Job serves You is for what he gets out of You. It's obvious. Look at how you've blessed him—sheep, cattle, wealth, and sons and daughters. Job doesn't care about You. He's after the blessings. If You were to take away the blessings, he would curse You to Your face."

So the book of Job begins with Satan's shaking his fist at God and throwing out a challenge. God was in a corner. Because He has conducted the great controversy from its very beginning in such a way that the devil can never accuse Him of being unfair, He had to let Satan try to prove his point.

So God withdrew His protection from Job's possessions, and the devil moved in with destruction. Overnight, everything Job had was taken away. He lost everything except his wife—and she should have been the first to go! Satan left her around, because she helped him in his plan by asking Job, "Why don't you just curse God and die?"

But Job remained faithful.

Then there came another day:

Again there was a day when the sons of God came to present themselves before the Lord, and Satan came also among them to present himself before the Lord. And the Lord said unto Satan, From whence comest thou? And Satan answered the Lord, and said, From going to and fro in the earth, and from walking up and down in it. And the Lord said unto Satan, Hast thou considered my servant Job, that there is none like him in the earth, a perfect and an upright man, one that feareth God, and escheweth evil? and still he holdeth fast his integrity, although thou movedst me against him, to destroy him, without cause (Job 2:1-3).

In effect God said to Satan, "You claim to be in charge there on the earth—and you managed to convince Me to let you try Job's commitment to Me, but now that you've taken everything from him, he still serves Me. He's still faithful. How do you explain it?"

Satan replied, "Skin for skin, yea, all that a man hath will he give for his life" (verse 4). In other words, Give me a chance! I need to touch him. Let me get just a little bit closer, and I'll have him.

So God said, "All right, go ahead. Try to prove your point—but spare his life."

So Satan arranged some boils. Job was terribly afflicted, in pain with boils from his head to his foot. His friends came by to comfort him, but they did a poor job of it. The rest of the book of Job records the dialogue between Job and his friends—and then between Job and God, as this man who loved God tried to understand what was happening in his life. He refused to turn his back on God but rather struggled to understand.

Now the story of Job is not just a history lesson. Let's bring it up to date.

Job, part 2

You go to your knees and you say, "I'm going to have a personal experience with God and seek to have a relationship with Him. I realize my need. I'm going to begin spending time with Him day by day."

At that point the devil shakes his fist at God and says, "Do you think this person is seeking You because he loves You? Not so. He is seeking You for selfish reasons. He wants his problems solved. He wants to escape hell. He wants to impress other people with his good life. He is seeking You, yes—but for the wrong reasons. If you'll just let me at him, I can prove it!"

So God says, "All right, you have permission to try and prove your point."

So the devil comes in with everything he has. He makes you the special object of temptation. He tries to get you to fail and fall and sin. He brings trouble, heartache, and pain. He reminds you of all your past failures. He tries to overburden you with guilt—and all for one purpose: he wants to get you to scrap your relationship with God because he knows that then he'll have you, and it will make God look bad as well.

Yes, our behavior often does get worse instead of better when we start developing a relationship with God. Because we do so many wrong things, we are tempted to forget about seeking Him. But one of the biggest proofs that you are a legalist is if you scrap your relationship with God because of your behavior! Seeking God should be a response of love, because of what Jesus has already done for you at the cross. We should be motivated to seek God for *His* sake, not just in order to control our behavior. Can you buy that?

Sometimes people say, "Yes, I understand that it's the devil who brings trials, afflictions, and persecution. But why would God allow me to live worse than I did before? That doesn't make sense!"

But God is in the business of showing us our need. He doesn't have to *manufacture* a need in order to have something to show us—we have plenty of needs already. He has only to arrange circumstances so that we become aware of what those needs are. Thus He is able to use even the attacks of Satan as a blessing to reveal to us that which it is good for us to know. Consider this inspired comment:

> Many who sincerely consecrate their lives to God's service are surprised and disappointed to find themselves, as never before, confronted by obstacles and beset by trials and perplexities. They pray for Christlikeness of character, for a fitness for the Lord's work, and they are placed in circumstances that seem to call forth all the evil of their nature. Faults are revealed of which they did not even suspect the existence. Like Israel of old, they question, "If God is leading us, why do all these things come upon us?" (*The Ministry of Healing*, p. 470).

The author goes on to say that "it is *because* God is leading them that these things come upon them" (p. 471). He is in control, even when He allows the enemy to test us to the limit.

God wants us to understand the waywardness of our own hearts so that we will feel our need of His strength instead of depending upon our own.

And in the process, God gives us the opportunity to vindicate Him from Satan's charges.

So, you see, when I began to seek God, and everything went wrong, and I quit seeking God because everything went wrong, whose side was I voting on? I was actually proving that the devil was right—and he sat back and laughed. Then one day it dawned on me that there is a great controversy going on, and God has to allow the enemy the opportunity to discourage us from seeking Him. And in the process, He is able to show us our own hearts and help us to understand what makes us tick. Then we can go to God in our weakness and begin to ask Him to give us the right motives and the determination to continue to seek Him regardless of circumstances.

The devil is not too smart!

If the devil were as intelligent as he ought to be after 6,000 years of practice, he would have left us alone after he got us to scrap our relationship with God the first time. If things had continued to go as well the rest of my life as they did the first few days after I quit seeking Jesus, the devil would have had me.

Perhaps a lack of intelligence is not Satan's problem. We are told that the highest evidence of nobility in a Christian is self-control. If that's true, and if the devil is the number one opposite of that, then the highest evidence of his *lack* of nobility would be a lack of self-control. So perhaps it is not a matter of Satan's not knowing any better. Perhaps it is more that he can't control himself. He knows that he *ought* to leave us alone, but he just can't *make* himself do it! He can hold off for a couple of weeks, and that's it. He just has to come at us again—just for fun this time. And in the end he drives us to our knees.

When the time finally comes that we tire of the on-again off-again relationship with God, and we keep on seeking Jesus regardless of what happens in our lives, then the scene is changed. Then we can join Job in playing a part in the vindication of God before the universe. What do you think it was like at the end of the book of Job, when Satan showed up in heaven for the third time? Imagine it with me.

God says, "Where did you come from?"

Satan says, "From walking to and fro on the earth. I'm in charge down there, you know."

And God says, "Have you considered my servant Job? In spite of everything you have done to him, he still maintains his integrity."

At this point the devil gets nervous. He begins kicking his feet in the dust. He has pulled out all the stops, and he has nothing left to try.

So God continues, "Is it possible that Job is seeking me because of love, because of what My Son did for him? Is it possible that he has learned to seek Me because of love, and not just for My blessings?"

And the devil is silenced.

Keep in mind that this conflict is repeated over every soul. Each one of us is given an opportunity to prove what our motives are in seeking after God. Just remember that Job wasn't left there among the ashes, covered with boils. The time came for healing, and in the end Job was blessed with far more than he had had before.

Job never knew what went on behind the scenes. We have been told the inside story, but Job wasn't. He was just invited to keep on trusting God—and we can do the same. We can make our choice to seek to know God through prayer and through the study of His Word day by day. We can choose to continue to seek Him every day until we see Him face to face, regardless of what happens in terms of blessings received.

"I wonder if she could use a horse"

When we lived in southern California, near La Sierra College, there was a little town called Norco that had more horses than people. You weren't even a decent citizen unless you had a couple of horses in your front yard. I think the mayor of Norco was a horse! And every teenage girl in town just *had* to have a horse of her own.

With that setting, let's suppose that one day my daughter comes to me and says, "Dad, I understand you're going on a trip."

"Yes."

"May I go along?"

I've been worried that there's some distance developing between my teenage daughter and me, so I'm thrilled at her request. I say to myself, "My teenage daughter? She still likes me!"

So I say, "Sure! You're welcome to come along."

So we start down the road, and after just a little while she says, "Dad?"

"Yes?"

"There's something I need to talk to you about."

"Is that right?"

"Yes. I need a horse."

Suddenly it becomes clear what she had in mind when she suggested coming along with me on this trip.

I say, "Sorry, you can't have a horse."

"Why not?"

"Well, we don't have any place to keep it. We can't afford it. We don't have anyone to take care of it when we're out of town. We don't know anything about horses." And so on. There are a lot of good reasons why she can't have a horse.

Things get really quiet. Time drags. We finish the trip with her looking out the window one way and me looking out the other way. When we get home, she goes off to bed without even saying goodnight.

Now let's back up and redo the story. She says, "You're going on a trip?"

"Yes."

"May I come along?"

"Yes." I'm excited. My teenage daughter—she still likes me!

We get into the car and start down the road. We talk. We laugh. She tells me some things that are happening at school. I share some things that are happening with my work. We discuss our joys and sorrows and dreams. She never even asks me for anything. We just talk. It's great!

At the end of the day we don't even know where the time has gone. We get back home, and she kisses me goodnight and goes off to bed. I go into the kitchen and say to my wife, "This is fantastic. My teenage daughter still likes me! I wonder if she could use a horse."

I don't want to bring God down to our level and make the illustration "stand on all fours," but because of the great controversy and the bigger issues involved, our motive in coming to God does make a difference.

When it has been proved to ourselves and to the universe and to all the forces of evil, that we have drawn a circle around our relationship with Jesus, and nothing will ever stop us from seeking fellowship with Him, then, and only then, can God pour out His blessings the way He longs to do.